Rob was born at the tball ever 1966, to a Welsh speaking working-class family in the coastal industrial town of Llanelli in South Wales. Rob's memoirs consider the highs and lows of living in such a close-knit community while trying to make sense of his sexuality.

With an overbearing mother and a fond and loving dad, who both left their imprint on his developing character, Rob gives a touchingly honest, sometimes tragic and often humourous account of his childhood and teenage years.

Rob has considered writing this book for many, many years. The confidence gained by finally facing up to the reality of his world has finally allowed his story to be told. He worked as a secondary school teacher, specialising in teaching Welsh as a first language for many years before moving into social care and is currently an education officer for 'Children Looked After' up in Gwynedd North Wales. A father to three wonderful girls whom he adores, he resides in the beautiful Quarry town of Llanfairfechan on the North Wales Coast with his wonderful husband David and his three boisterous hounds.

I wrote this book in *memory* of my father Elwyn (aka Jim),
who taught me how to treat other people with respect, kindness
and a smile, and for my girls Sioned, Luned and Anwen,
who are everything to me.

Rob Jewell

ALL SHOW OFF

Memories of an Odd Ball's Childhood in Llanelli

AUSTIN MACAULEY PUBLISHERS™
LONDON • CAMBRIDGE • NEW YORK • SHARJAH

Copyright © Rob Jewell 2022

The right of Rob Jewell to be identified as author of this work has been asserted by the author in accordance with sections 77 and 78 of the Copyright, Designs and Patents Act 1988.

All rights reserved. No part of this publication may be reproduced, stored in a retrieval system, or transmitted in any form or by any means, electronic, mechanical, photocopying, recording, or otherwise, without the prior permission of the publishers.

Any person who commits any unauthorised act in relation to this publication may be liable to criminal prosecution and civil claims for damages.

A CIP catalogue record for this title is available from the British Library.

ISBN 9781398457874 (Paperback)
ISBN 9781398457881 (ePub e-book)

www.austinmacauley.com

First Published 2022
Austin Macauley Publishers Ltd®
1 Canada Square
Canary Wharf
London
E14 5AA

I want to thank my husband David for having the patience to listen to me waffling on about the content of this book for far too long and in doing so, interrupting his sci-fi fixation for once! To the moon and beyond!

Thanks are also due to my publishers, who believed in me when I had doubts myself!

And finally, a great, big 'thank you' to those people both alive and dead, who were instrumental to the memory of my experiences and recollections.

– Rob Jewell
Summer 2019

Introduction

So why write this book?

OK, if I'm completely honest, since I've been quite ill just before my half-century, at the end of 2016, I realised that I hadn't ever got around to passing on the stories of my childhood to my children; that cluster of experiences and characters from my past that have "helped" me become the person that their father is today.

With heart, lung and liver problems, I'm convinced that I'm not coming off this planet alive and that someone is certainly targeting me somewhere and I have felt the need to get things down pretty quickly. If and when the day comes for the next generation of my family, my girls will be able to repeat the funny peculiar stories of my early life.

Memories of a childhood in the late 60s and 70s Llanelli are considered within, though they'll possibly be of no consequence to others, I hope that my girls find them of interest. This entanglement of belonging and of being is what has made me who I am and how I am.

I've never written a book before, though I've created one many times and at many stages of my life in my head. English is not even my mother tongue. Welsh has and always will be more comfortable for me, though I'll try to make Dr Martin

Rhys, my English teacher, who I both revered and feared at Ysgol y Strade, proud.

The childhood memories noted here are true from my perspective. Any factual mistakes are there because that's how I remember them happening. None of the content is aimed at upsetting anyone, but I'm sure it will. "Que sera, sera," as Myngu Norman used to say.

I've kept some personal stuff out, which if included, would create a fuss and shadow all my recollections. I've lived with them long enough as it is, though they may surface unintentionally in my writing.

Enjoy the reading and enjoy the memories – I've enjoyed organising them into some sort of order, so that my children may understand why I am as I am and for people that know me to have the option of crossing the road when they see me heading towards them!

Lastly, after you've read the book, consider this quote from Somerset Maugham (1874–1965) in his memoirs *The Summing Up* in 1938: "There is an impression abroad that everyone has it in him to write one book; but if by this is implied a good book then the impression is false."

– Diolch
– Rob Jewell
Summer 2019

Part 1
Community's Influences

Chapter 1
Coming into This World and Finding My Place in the Family.

Aunty Muriel across the road was the first to greet me into this big wide world. Eight days before Christmas in the year of England's treasured World Cup win. I'm surprised that I wasn't named Nobby or Bobby or Alf or Gordon or any of the other players of that winning team. My parents settled for Robert Ashley which was as English as it could get! I was apparently born after another Robert Ashley who'd been born some months earlier down the road and Mam liked the name! To be honest it could have been worse – as she liked the name Roger too! The connotations of which would've been very unfortunate, in the developing circumstances of my personal life.

I hope that Jenny the shop had her tongue firmly in her cheek when she told Mam, who'd wheeled me there in a white metal pram with rosebuds on it after Amanda up the road, "He'll be Prime Minister with a name like that!"

I was born in the parlour of our house in High Street, Llanelli, as was the fashion at the time. Only my sister, being the first born was born in Glasfryn, Felinfoel Road and both my brother and me were home births. I was the third born and

Mam and Dad had already had a daughter and a son so didn't worry what sex I'd be as long as I was healthy.

I heard many times that "they" were worried that I'd be born "deformed", as my head felt too big in the womb. In the days before ultra-sound, there was a fair bit of guesswork to it. Who "they" were I never got to know, but if "they" had only looked at my mother and my grandfather, Dycu Jack, her father, they'd have realised that large heads come naturally in our family.

It was a quarter to one when I finally made an appearance to the awaiting crowds, just in time for my first lunch as a 10-pound 3-ounce baby. I'm full of theories, and I've always thought that being born so near lunchtime, set the scene for a lifetime of loving and craving food and fighting the guilt of having an ever-expanding waistline. I was a "lunchtime baby" from the start. Having welcomed me, my dad went off to his afternoon shift in the local tin plate works.

As a child, I was obsessed with incubators and my question to my mam was always, "Was I in an incubator when I was born? Her answer was always the same,"Incubator? They'd have needed a glasshouse for you!"

I don't actually remember much from my first day – just that there was another mouth to feed and money was tight and that we were different from the other kids. In time, I'd find out that we were "the welshies" or "Welsh cakes" as the kids at the back called us from the safety of their street on the other side of the railway line. Thinking back, I don't believe that they were any different to us, but we spoke Welsh and we were seen as "different" by the other kids in this cosmopolitan Llanelli of the late '60s!

We were handy as the little "welshies" when it came to New Year activities of course and welcoming in the New Year with our traditional Welsh welcome songs – "C'lennig, c'lennig, bore dydd y Calan, Nawr yw'r amser i gasglu'r arian". "Happy New Year to You and all your happy family! The New Year's in, the old year's out – Happy New Year to you all." Me and my brother could make a small fortune if we timed it nice and early in High Street on New Year's Day as everyone knew us, though my sister didn't ever have the welcome that was reserved for dark-haired boys who were said to bring luck to the household. Collecting all the coins we could before 12, so that we could go off to Woolworths then to spend it all on pick and mix.

My childhood was plagued by illness as I remember. Nothing too serious just constant gripes. A "winter baby" was always given as the reason. Always feeling bad – a snobby nose and sore throat to match and first to catch whatever was going and the last to get rid of it too.. A clear memory from these early years, is having a hard left sleeve on all my jumpers and coats as I couldn't blow my nose, so constantly used my sleeve to wipe my snout!

One of the earliest memories I've got is of having a love of fruit pastilles. Though I didn't understand at the time, that this had been planted in my mind from a very early age and that it had also led to a string of events that came about after my dad dropped me from a great height!

Apparently, I'd been climbing up his chest like a baby, and when I reached his shoulder, I dropped over the side and down the other side and right onto my big head. But I didn't just fall. Oh no I fell on one of Dad's new concrete skirtings in the middle room and ended up in Llanelli General for a few days and apparently all my visitors brought me fruit pastilles as per my mam's suggestion.

Poor Dad. He got so much stick off everyone; my sister having locked herself in the bathroom, refusing to come out as he'd "killed" her baby brother and my brother, having been sent to stay with my myngu Susan – she having noticed in her infinite wisdom to tell my mam and dad that my brother had a squint. This resulted in National Health glasses and a patch for a long time.

****

I had quite a lonely childhood, to be honest. As the youngest, with a sister six years older than me and a brother four years older, it meant that I very often remember playing by myself. I quickly learnt to entertain myself and to be comfortable in my own company, as I didn't have a choice. This skill has helped me through some difficult life patches, many times. At 52 years of age, I can still find ways of entertaining myself and should I find myself alone and far from home, I look out for a TKMaxx every time, or a TJMaxx as it's known in New York!

I've often spoken to my sister about the fact, that even though we were three kids in a family with the same Mam and Dad, we were brought up individually, independent of each other but under Mam's full control. We would never dream of depending on each other but were slowly and individually dependent on Mammy. We were brought up not to rely on and trust each other, but to tell on each other to earn favour with Mammy. Mam was the Centre point for any confidence, or any information sharing. To be completely honest, there was no chance of changing that, that's just how it was and how it was meant to be. I often hear of families, who have great get-togethers, where they all enjoy each other's company. We had no chance of that. The differences emphasised between us at a very young age, and that lack of trust is still very evident to this day.

It's so true what Armisted Maupin wrote in his book, Logical Family: A Memoir "Sooner or later, though, no matter where in the world we live, we must join the diaspora, venturing beyond our biological family to find our logical one, the one that actually makes sense for us."

The biological family I got, hasn't ever proved to have much influence or emotional support for me as I grew up and the importance of friends and even neighbours, has proved their worth across the years though they may have changed at different periods of my life.

To take this a step further, I have spent my entire life battling against the judgement of members of my family, especially my mam. Nothing quite right or quite good enough. I've never really been able to please however hard I've tried, and that insecurity is shown in my character still. I'm still as critical of myself, as I was told I should be when growing up all those years ago. If it's not my weight it's the way I talk, or the way that I dress. Self-image smashed to pieces from an early age so as to deny me my true character. Unable to receive any praise, and always trying to please.

I used to dread taking my school class pictures home. "Why aren't you in the front like so and so…?" "You are always in the back. Backward coming forward, you are!"

Or if I somehow had pushed my overweight carcass to the front, I'd get, "Who do you think you are then, pushing your way to the front?!" I just couldn't win though I tried and tried.

When I was a secondary school teacher, the kids that I taught used to tell me to stop putting myself down. They claimed that I was always so hard on myself. That I only concentrated on my failures. But, I had learnt from as long as I can remember, that by knocking myself, it made being knocked by others easier to cope with, and those that said that they, "were only saying", apparently only doing so to keep me grounded?

If I gained weight, I'd have to face, "You've gone terribly fat!" And if I'd dare challenge the comment, I'd be told, "I'm only saying!" and then if I went on a strict diet, as I inevitably tried, would get, "Don't think you look smart like that! You're looking terribly thin". That "terribly" was always there as a true sign of how I was seen whatever I tried to do. As I've said, I just couldn't win!

Nothing was good enough and could never please some people and if I tried to reason the response, I found myself banging my head against an emotional wall of denial of other people's feelings.

At this stage of my life and long past what might have been considered my prime, I'm a father to three fantastic girls, who receive little to no judgement, whatever their size, fashion sense or career choice and I've tried hard to protect them from the negative comments of some members of my birth family, who should be congratulating them and praising their kindness and celebrating their achievements instead of looking desperately for their faults. I openly and proudly celebrate my girls' successes and contrary to the old idea of never praising your own, I concentrate on their strengths, and their lovely nature, and more than that, they know that I'll be there for them to support them for as long as I breathe.

Married for the second time to a man that I adore, after giving in to who I really was for so long, and after hating myself and judging myself all the while, I'm starting to see the Robert Ashley that I should have seen years ago – his strengths as well as his weaknesses. I've also realised the need to say farewell to the constant negativity of some of my family, who seem to want nothing more than a reason to talk about me in their nastiness with each other to add an element of excitement to their otherwise uneventful lives!

My dad was the saving grace for me as a child and throughout my life. The most positive attachment that I had in my early life was Daddy. Not a well-educated man, but a man whose general knowledge and interest in things was incredibly rich. In another age, my dad could've been a historian, such was his love, and my own as well as at least one of my daughters in all things historical.

I was always closer to my dad than my mam. In the evenings, we used to play cards, play chess and chat and chat and chat. Those of you who know me, know that I can talk for Wales and have a genuine interest in other people. Well, I got all that from my dad. We had respect for each other, appreciated each other, never argued and in his final years, we learnt to support each other best we could to make sense of this crazy world.

In the evenings, with my mother and brother having gone to their beds since nine, we'd settle to watch a film together on the telly. If that film became quite sexual in nature, my father would say, "Right, I'll go and sort the dog out for bed, see what else is on Robs" – every time!

When my sister was working for her O levels, me and Dad used to go to Gorseinon for extra Maths and French lessons. We'd spend the hour, while waiting for her, walking around and chatting non-stop, and if we did buy from the sweet shop, Dad would buy polos every time.

Dad was a "Labour" man through and through. Even his blood was red – proof if ever there was proof needed, that that was what the Country needed. Dad was a man born and bred in Llanelli, and true to form was a true working-class man. As I grew up and started considering myself all-knowing, I'd joke with him that he would support a donkey if it had a red rosette on it. His answer was always the same, "Aye, I would as long as it was a Labour donkey!"

I'd like to think that I've had my care for others and my love for my children from my thoughtful, kind and very dear father, as he had had from his mam and dad too. Losing my dad, as it came in the middle of the failure of my first marriage, was an experience that I wouldn't wish on my worst enemy. To this day, I still look for a nice fairisle jumper for my dad for Christmas, before realising that he's no longer with us. Having said this, I also feel that he's always with me. I see him appear in my character and the way that I try to treat others. My political rantings are straight off my dad, though in Wales my colour's changed from red and the fact that I have immense pride in my children like he always had in his. He never knew Facebook but had he done, he'd have been as militant a keyboard politician as I am.

I think that my sister liked having a little brother to look after when I was a little boy. As the eldest of three, I think that the pressure on her must have been great. Parents' and family expectations were always so high, and my sister so very shy as a young girl. I adored my sister but could be a pest to her as well. She was six years older than me, and I was always the little boy in her eyes, and I could argue that I'm still seen like that. She was the eldest and received so much affection laced with criticism and expectation that she should help around the house. She had to experience life as the eldest, doing everything for the first time. Her relationship with my brother was competitive for as long as I can remember; he like my sister, trying to make their own way through Society and both, normally, trying their best to please my mother.

It's really strange having two people who share the same parents as you, but who respond so differently from each other. I've always thought that my sister was like my dad's side of the family, and my brother's character more like my mam's side. Yes, it is "sides" I would say too. As if the two sides were competing against each other. Two sides of the same family. I've always known that me and my sister were on my father's side, while my brother always responded better to mam's side. I can also say that I was a daddy's boy, and I still am, though the poor dab's been dead 10 years. My brother, in my mind, behaved more like my mother and her family. My sister's more difficult to read, a combination of both sides at different times.

What is interesting, is that my mam and dad were very different characters when I was growing up, and my sister and brother had very different experiences with their parenting. Mam always said that I was a "cooler", like my dad.

With regards to my brother, I remember trying so hard to be like him when I was small. My brother was always right, always managed to make people laugh by doing silly things, and always seemed popular with the extended family and of course, could do no wrong in Mam's eyes. My brother had the power of an older brother over me, and thinking back, Dad would always try to make sure that it didn't overpower me and tried to keep him in his place. My brother could do and say things that would often wind my father up, though my mam always supported him. As I got older, I remember starting to get fed up with my brother's "nonsense", and started looking to my sister for guidance. Looking up to her, allowed me to do well at school, and follow a career in teaching as she had done, even to the extent of studying the same subject at the same university. There was a great pressure for me to do well at school, and Mam obviously saw potential in me somewhere, though she'd never have praised it at the time. Even as a forty something year old leading Educational training at a conference, I'd have to put up with my mam's negativity. When trying to impress her by telling her that I was going to be earning a sizeable amount of money for one day's professional training that day, her comment was as negative as ever, "Who'd want to pay to listen to you?" Of course, as usual, she was "only saying!"

My brother didn't make much effort at school and unlike my sister who always tried her best. My sister and my brother's influence was already on the school when I arrived there, and it was difficult at the start, to not be compared to them both. As comparisons go, I think I was compared favourably to my sister in junior school, but also managed to establish myself in my own right.

With such an unusual surname, everyone knew who we were, and everyone also remembered us for the good and the bad things that we did. We had no chance of keeping a low profile as Jewells!

Chapter 2
Growing Up as a Member of High Street Society

Everybody knew everybody in the street where I was brought up. A close community of terraced houses facing each other, with their front doors straight to the pavement. Each one had its own part of the pavement to keep clean, and the nets always needed to be white and tidy and evenly distributed across the windows. God forbid that someone should allow standards to slip, and they'd be constantly judged on these essential criteria. Everyone knew us, of course, because we were different from the other kids in the street. As naturally fluent Welsh speakers, we went to Chapel and Sunday school and didn't attend the local primary.

I wasn't allowed to step over the doorstep of number 46, to go playing. It was a dangerous world out there, beyond the haven of our home, and I didn't mix with the local kids until I was 12. Until then, I was kept in and only allowed to play out the back on the railway bank behind the house. Our house backed onto the mainline from Swansea to West Wales. Our garden was a mixture of glass house to one side and lots of roses to the other side, with a middle path. Later on, it contained a shed at the bottom too, to keep budgies. Dad had adapted the old toilet at the bottom of the garden. My brother was very similar to Dycu Jack in many ways, and they shared a love of budgies. He had everything he could possibly need for those budgies, before realising that he was allergic to the dust with the budgies cages so that my dad had to take over their care, though he had little desire to do so.

I can remember Daddy's glasshouse every summer – me as the youngest getting the biggest tomato and eating it like an apple. That taste is still embedded in my mind, and cine film was taken at the time, of me as a little boy with summer clothes and sandals, coming out of the glasshouse, all proud with a massive oversized tomato.

I spent my early Summers wandering that bank. The very bank, by the way, became famous in the Railway Riots of 1911. I used to make up songs as I wandered aimlessly, singing at full volume to my heart's content, as there was no one around me. I'd create pathways in the bank, though I mostly stuck to the rule of not going all the way down to the main line. We'd have all sorts of cargo trains coming past, and the guardsmen on the back carriage were always extremely friendly. Imagine, if you will that famous scene out of the Railway Children, but only me and minus the long hair, the sticking out teeth and the white pinafores. I'd walk at the top of the bank too, chatting with the old people, busy in their long back gardens, and always dreaming of how life would turn out for me when I was older.

There was one old lady who lived down the bottom of the road called Mrs Simms, and she even remembered the riots as a Young girl. As a child, I always thought that she was very very old, and spoke with a West Country accent, not so different from my Dycu Bill. She'd lived most of her adult life in High Street I think. She called me Bobby, at a time when everyone else called me Robert. I used to love going down there to see her. She always had time for a chat. She was helped by Edwin her gardener and companion. He was a lovely old man, resembling a tramp in his oversized coat and flat cap with a trouser belt to keep the coat together. She seemed to love his company. He didn't live with her but had a house behind Orsis cafe in Station Road, which to all intent and purposes looked derelict. When he died, rumour has it, that they found a lot of money in the house and that he was worth a fortune!

Another neighbour who was always in her garden was "Licky locky". I never ever knew her name, but she was often in her garden, and depending on her mood, would either tell me off for passing on the bank or summons me for a chat. She was always talking, and I'm reminded of her every time I see snapdragons in a garden. By holding the flower you can make it talk, just like old "Licky Locky" whose garden was full of them.

I also played with the smaller kids next door, but enjoyed the company of adults more, was great friends with the "Witty" sisters and was gutted when they moved away as they had their gramps' old shed to play with and even had an attic in their house that they could use.

Next door the other way, was a family of a sister and two brothers. We would hear Arthur clearing his chest in the back kitchen every morning – a sure sign that the day had begun like a character straight out of Dylan Thomas's Under Milk Wood. Cath, the sister was a really nice lady. We'd hear her singing to herself as she worked in the kitchen, and Arwyn the other brother was a "character". In a world, that was miles apart from what we take for granted today, and Arwyn preferring the company of men as he did, he was the talk of the local gossiping wives and mothers. He was a Good man, willing to help anyone. He knew everyone's business but because he was "queer" was not seen as favourably as other people by Society at the time.

His "friends" were well known to us all too, as we'd sometimes hear them, in a drunken state, calling up to him in the street at night. What was really odd about that time, was that camp people were accepted on one level within society, as people to gossip with on the street or in the market, but god forbid that the way they conducted their love lives should ever be seen as acceptable. In that society, I grew up and I learnt from a very early age, not to draw too much attention to myself in case I ended up being judged as Arwyn and many like him were judged. Of course, television was full of camp catchphrases designed to give the general population a good laugh at homosexuality's expense. "I'm free", "shut that door," and "what a gay day" all being acceptable though you wouldn't dare say that you supported their right to love who they wanted. Mam's stark warning, "Keep away from him next door!" as if a man who was gay was bound to want to sexually assault a young boy. People know by now, that children who are sexually abused are normally abused by family members not strangers.

High Street like Llanelli in general, was a close-knit, friendly and comfortable community to be part of on the one hand, as long as you followed life's pattern – down to Stradey to watch the rugby, go through school, get work locally, enjoy a pint of Buckley's down the pub, find a girlfriend, marry and have kids, but a cruel Society for those who didn't fit that pattern, on the other hand. Mam and many like her would see them as "odd balls", and saw it as her duty to protect me from them, though I think she knew deep down that I was becoming an"odd ball" too. Talking about gay people was never seen in a positive light in our house. One of the First of many swear words that I remember hearing at home was "Bumboy!" and aimed, not at me, but at my brother by my sister during one of so many quarrels. The ultimate offence!

I kept my confused sexuality to myself as I grew up. These days I'm happy to report, that I'm comfortable in my own skin, but years ago, and with others' response to the notion so horrendous, and not being comfortable to have any consideration for sex, but being called every poof under the sun by other boys at school, I preferred to completely avoid any notion of sex in any shape or form.

Our Society would laugh at someone who didn't like rugby or a good game of football, and then if you add folk dancing and singing soprano in duets with Joanne Phillips or Cerys Davies, then my personal shame at the time is complete. I tried so hard not to be me, to avoid drawing attention to myself for fear of being shown to be different, but when you're a big-boned fat boy, and "all show off" as Mam would say, then you don't have much choice.

While the other boys played summer cricket (the most tedious game that I ever had the misfortune to be forced to play, as I was left-handed and couldn't catch or throw a ball) at lunchtime in junior school, I would be content playing elastics with a select group of girls who didn't seem to mind me. My thanks go out to Catherine Morris and Ffion Thomas for their radical attitude in making a friend of me at the time.

Children around where I lived all went to a different school to me, and I only ever saw my school friends in term time.

I'd need to entertain myself and our swing in the back garden was essential to that enjoyment for a long time.

Otherwise, me and my brother would play chip shop through the large bathroom window which would open out to the garden and we'd sell chips and all sorts of things that we'd have created from the earth and mud in the garden. The chips were always made out of toilet paper, and food was always an important part of any play every time.

Once, when Mammy was out, and Daddy was looking after us, we were playing in the back garden, and my brother convinced me that it would be fun to change the colour of my hair. Seconds later, I was running into the back kitchen with half a tin of tangerine emulsion all over my head. Dad nearly had a fit and while shouting at my brother, had my head under the tap in the wash up to get rid of it before Mammy came home.

In the summer, and only a bath twice a week, it was a treat to stand outside the kitchen window in our bathers, while Mam put the hose pipe on us. A different era for sure, but we enjoyed the fun of it and appreciated the silliness of soaking each other in the heat. Another treat was when the man from Alpine pops delivered to the house. We'd always had Llan pop or Corona but these pops were very different. Unheard-of flavours and very reasonable. There was no such thing as sugar-free at the time, and we enjoyed the additives and all the colourings.

Mammy often used to buy a pint of cockles from the woman who'd come around the door to door selling what she'd just picked, and then we'd make our way to the market then, for laverbread to eat them with onions, bacon, mash potato and baked beans.

Living near the sea was something that I remember being grateful for, even as a child, and as I got older, Llanelli beach was my sanctuary. Sitting alone and allowing me to try and make sense of my world while staring out to sea was essential to me.

Another wonderful memory that I hold dear to me, was when we heard neighbours in the street shouting, "The horses are coming, the horses are coming!" and everyone used to go in and head to the parlour, carefully drawing those White nets to the side, ready for the charging wild horses. These were the wild horses of Penclawdd, and the kids from Morfa, Seaside or Bwlch y Gwynt used to lead them over the estuary on a low tide, then leave them stranded there. Last time I was down in Llanelli, in what is now the super-rich Machynys, there were still wild horses grazing around the unspoilt areas.

When someone died in our street, everyone would close their front curtains out of respect, until after the funeral. I'm sure, that it was a superstition about keeping evil spirits out of the house, and as I got older, I realised that the High street community was starting to disappear when fewer and fewer people closed their curtains as the population changed.

Our street represented the society in full, the sinners and the saints, all living alongside each other behind closed doors. We had Hector Bowen, father of the famous and local boy did good singer Kenneth Bowen, who had sung at Prince Charles's Investiture in and as so many of Llanelli's residents at the time, so proud of their loyalty to the royalty. Mam and Aunty Muriel organised the street corner party in 1969, and

I've just found a picture from that event with me as a two-year-old, dressed up like a robin red breast.

Mam organised the street committee for the Silver Jubilee celebrations too in 1977, and after a party in the yard of the old Dewi Sant school in the afternoon, we had a Good old knees up in the evening, Street closed, and the union jacks and the cut-out crowns in our front windows; parlour window open and stereo blasting music from an era that young and old could enjoy.

A few houses up from Mr Bowen, there was an elderly lady who by all accounts had spent some time in jail, for giving illegal abortions to desperate women, at a time when abortions were illegal up until 1967. Much talk about the infamous Mandy Rice Davies who was from Llanelli, having allegedly recommended a friend to come all the way from London to give Lil in High Street a visit to end her troubles. Tragically, she died on the way back on the train back to London, and Lil's fate was sealed.

Amongst the other local celebrities that we had in Llanelli, were the Langs who lived across the road. The Lang family were famous for their laverbread, with a stall In Llanelli Market selling it it buy the scoop full. We were multi-cultural, even then, with not one but two Germans living amongst us. Heinz and his Welsh wife Rose and the children were there, as well as "John the German" and his Welsh family who lived there. Good people with an accent so far removed from the rest of us, and though it was twenty years since the war's end, their presence was still noted and talked about often.

We had an "unconventional tobacconist on the corner of High Street with Lakefield Road. Aunty Phil lived there, and her large side window an excellent look out for unsuspecting travellers to town and back. She was an extremely fit and healthy woman, who was forever walking down the beach, swimming and keeping fit. Unfortunately, she also used to provide a service of selling single fags and packets of cigarettes to underage children. When I got old enough to try smoking, I kept well away from Aunty Phil for fear of getting caught there by my mam.

We had two corner shops in our street; Peter's the shop at the bottom and the imaginatively named Top shop at the top of our street on the other side. Marion and Vic who owned the top shop seemed terribly posh when I was a child, and I loved going there to buy penny sweets or even a custard slice or a corned beef pasty. If I'm honest, I could write a whole chapter on food in this book of memories. I live in Bangor, and at 52 years of age, I still hunt for the best place to sell pasties, since Morris Bros from Cwm y glo retired, and saddened that the choice is reducing while my waistline continues to increase.

A bizarre Memory that survives to this day, is of me going up to top shop with a message off my mam presented in a sealed envelope. I remember queueing to deliver this message to an unsuspecting Vic with all the mystery of a ransom note. When he opened the note he turned a bright shade of red, put whatever was requested in a brown paper bag and off I went. Dr White's pads were in the bag, obviously needed at home, and at the time I had no idea what they were or why they had created such an embarrassment to Vic.

Both shops sold a bit of everything, to be honest, but we bought our bread from Peter's shop. A John Rees batch it was every time, and everyone nagging for the crust with shir gar butter full of salt. I learnt from an early age how to cut a toc for myself, even though I'd frighten everyone with my left-handed ways! A "queen's toc" was always called for if Mam wasn't well. A toc sliced so thin that you could almost see through it. We went off John Rees 'bread at one stage though, as Mam found a fag stump in a loaf. Down she went to Peter's shop, threatening all sorts of "weights and measures" on the Bakery. John Rees the Baker himself delivered our hamper of fresh things, by way of apology, and as it was coming up to my birthday, I was given a free birthday cake. He must have thought that he'd please me with a large iced sponge cake with nuts around the side and a football scene complete with goals and football characters on the top. The boys who'd been invited to my party seemed to like it, but I could only see the merit of a big cake to eat. And like so many early birthday parties which were single-sexed, I ended up on my own eating cake while the boys all played around me.

Then, like many many other times, I didn't need to be told that I was different from the other boys. I knew it, and it was obvious to all. The thought of playing football made me feel bad; I was fat and couldn't contemplate changing in front of the others, and had never had any desire to kick a ball of any shape. My own shape didn't help matters and, "he's a good size for a prop forward," uttered by Mam's friends who we'd see in town only added to my misery. I have never been able to stand by a urinal to pee, and I'll wait until a cubicle becomes available every time. Mam would sometimes say, "What have you got that's so special that you've got to hide it then?'

Other comments that made my skin crawl were, "I'm sure that this one's breaking hearts!" especially as I was intent on hiding my true feelings, and Mam's response was equally cringe-worthy, "This one's got no interest in girls!"

****

We had a dog and cats and a tortoise sharing our garden. Animals in the house were strictly forbidden, except for the dog who was allowed in the back kitchen to sleep in his cwtch by the Rayburn. Whiskey, the dog, was a white toy poodle chosen by my brother and extremely ill-suited from the start to an un-pampered lifestyle in a busy family with young children. He was called Whiskey as Mam's sister, Aunty Ann, had a dog called Shandy at the time. Unfortunately, Shandy didn't last long after Whiskey arrived, as Mam bought him reduced mincemeat and it poisoned him. Whiskey wasn't a particularly friendly pet and learnt to fear and hate the kitchen brush that Mam would use to shoo him out in the mornings. Only Daddy was allowed to stroke him below the neck, and only Dad could bathe him too. He would snarl at everyone else, and Mam would have daily run-ins with him over his position by the Rayburn. He lived till he was 17 and did mellow in his final years. Still couldn't stroke him below his head though!

Tiger and Fluff were the two cats. I strongly believe that my brother must've named the cats as Tiger was all Black and didn't resemble a tiger at all! Fluff was a grey and white ball of fur. These would've been Duport Steel Works' cats, as Dycu Jack used to bring them over after ending his afternoon shift. They weren't indoor cats. Semi-feral and living outdoors, they had never met a vet in their lives. As a little boy, my memory is always of seeing Tiger with her litter in the big glasshouse ready to scram for anyone considering taking a kitten. But not all cats were allowed to live. At a very different age, and with money tight, and the family needing more things than taking a cat to the vet, Dad would have to drown the cats when they were born. It's no wonder that Tiger learnt to protect her kittens.

Tortie was the tortoise's imaginative name, and we had him for many years. We attempted to put him in a box for the winter only once, and that was the year he didn't wake up. Tortie followed his own path for years, and would often disappear as the weather changed, only to reappear come March.

And last but by no means least we had the budgies. Though I say we, they were always my brother's especially when it came to selling them. My brother's early attempts at copying Richard Branson's success in my opinion, and Dycu Jack would profit from selling to my brother too, however old or infirm they happened to be.

Chapter 3
Working, "Stop Fortnight" and Family Holidays

Both Mam and Dad worked while I was a little boy. Mam was a dinner lady at Copperworks, the school next door to ours. To a child who had learnt to totally rely on my mam from an early age, seeing her walking around with other children and not being able to be with her was truly painful for me and managed to create all sorts of insecurity in my head. When I started full-time school, Mam started work as a school cleaner. She'd be working every school night after school closed, and Dad used to pick me up from school most days. When Daddy was working the afternoon shift, someone else would fetch me. Mammy would always prepare tea, and Daddy would warm it up. I can still remember Dad's food after school and if I was offered the choice of meals on my last supper ever, I'd settle for tinned salmon and home chips with two rounds of bread and butter. Sometimes, I'd get to go to my mam's school while she was working. I'd get to play at being a teacher, writing on the blackboards in the different classes, without thought to one day being a teacher for real. Mam would have to make sure that everything was spot on for the next day's learning for the little ones at Stebonheath.

Mam took great pride in her work. The brass was always gleaming on the door handles, the floors polished 'til you could see your face in them and always ready to be dirtied again the following day.

Dad worked in Trostre tin plate works on shifts. They ranged from the morning shift 6 a.m. – 2 p.m., the afternoon shift 2 p.m. – 10 p.m., or the night shift 10 p.m. – 6 a.m. Mam didn't like it when Dad worked the night shift. She was frightened to be in the house overnight without him. Daddy used to go at half-past nine at night and Mam would need all the doors locked and the house locked up 'til the morning. No one was to go out and it was time for bed. It was a hell of a thing to have to go to bed so early in the middle of summer, while the sky was still blue and the daylight coming in through the curtains.

Thinking back, I can understand my mother's nervousness, remembering that we'd had a murder on High Street when I was a baby. An old lady living alone in number 16, had been killed by the coal man's helper. Apparently, he'd seen her reaching for her tin of money to pay the coalman, and had decided that he wanted that for himself. That same evening, he came back up the bank behind our houses and went in through the scullery. She'd tried to fend him off and protect her money and paid for it with her life as he'd strangled her with her own stockings and left her dead body under the kitchen table. He escaped back over the wall, across the bank and followed the line to the station where he caught a train for London. Mam remembered it as it was such a horribly wet, stormy night and no one was out the back to see anyone walking past.

He was caught, of course, but it put the fear of god into High street's residents, with the realisation that such a thing could happen in such a close-knit community. I remember the description given of the murdered old lady. A lovely quiet old lady, respectable, who'd keep her pavement clean at all times, who made sure that her nets were always clean and tidy, and who kept herself to herself. The perfect attributes of the ideal citizen in Llanelli at the time.

****

There'd be a lot of excitement as we packed for our holidays. Sleeping bags piled under us in the back seat of the car, a full boot of bags of clothes and food for a week's holiday. You'd swear that it was impossible to buy corn flakes and coffee where we were going! We'd always be perched on top of the sleeping bags, no safety belt anywhere near us, and always me in the middle to try and lessen any bickering which could so easily start up between the warring factions that were my sister and brother.

I remember going many times straight after school term finished. School reports were given out to come home on that last day, and the disappointment surrounding my sister's 11+ failure spoilt the beginning of one holiday because she knew and we all knew that she'd worked hard and something very wrong had happened. This would also mean that she'd be separated from her friends. Years later, my sister was telling someone at college that they'd all had to write their answers in pencil at school, and was told that the exam papers that came in from the schools were always in ink. I'd be extremely foolish to suggest that adults had any vested interest in securing the desired outcome for children of more influential families, but somehow something wasn't quite right about the process. Whatever happened at the time, my sister passed her 13+Exams and got the chance to further succeed at the grammar school for girls. For my brother, there was little surprise that he didn't pass, as he didn't work and concentrated even less though he had "plenty upstairs" according to his teachers and this time the holidays proceeded as a way to forget about it all at the start of the six weeks off.

When I was young, we almost always went to either Pendine or Tenby, but sometimes to both at different times of the year.

Every Easter, we'd stay in a caravan by the ice cream factory that Eric Eynon owned in Pendine. The old Windsor Creameries. It was a lovely old blue and cream caravan, which was very comfortable apart from the hundreds of plastic flowers and cheap '70s ornaments that were in every nook and crany. The caravan was called "Susan" as was the fashion to give a human name to your Holiday home at the time. "Don't touch anything," were Mammy's first words every time, "in case you break something". But it was very difficult not to touch anything, especially if it was raining and much less to do indoors. We weren't allowed to "play with the Windows" either, even if it was boiling inside. "Out to play", we should go in nice weather. My brother did dare open a window once, and as Mam said, the window broke. The same was true when we walked around endless Holiday shops selling the same "wish you were here" gifts, something which I still do on holidays to this day. The lack of variety, quite comforting. They were normally owned by the same people, but it was something to spend your Holiday money on, and a way for

Mam to keep control of us," Nice to handle, Nice to hold, but if you break it, consider it SOLD!" stamped on my Memory still, and I still walk around the shops like a soldier arms down and no touching!

I remember Whiskey the dog, coming with us down to Pendine once. We must have gone for the day. I must have been very young because he was also very young. One of our family enjoyments was walking around the rocks when the tide was in, but this time we had the added issue of the dog who wasn't as ready to listen and obey my mam as we were. The poor dab jumped straight into the sea when we started our walk. That day Whiskey realised that he could paddle furiously and stay afloat, but only just, as the waves washed over his head and he was bound to drown. I was in hysterics, for fear of losing him to the sea, but Dad managed to save him with my little fishing net. He was terrified and was shaking the whole way back to the car wrapped in my dad's cardigan.

Before the days of sunscreen, and sheltering from the sun, we were all, on Holiday, to get the best colour suntan that we could and calamine lotion was essential to pack before going. Sometimes Dad would still be at work and Mam would look after us on her own. Together in a confined space, we must've been horrendous for Mammy. My sister and brother couldn't agree on anything and the "constant bickering" as Mam would say. Got us all down. By the time that Dad had finished work and come down to join us, we were all burnt raw and as painful as the devil himself. But the biggest joke was, that after a day in the sun, Daddy would be as brown as a berry, and look much more sun-drenched than the rest of us. "That's the gypsy in my blood," my dad would say. Dad was indeed a darker complexion than us, but have managed to avoid the hereditary red hair from both sides of the family, we were happy enough to settle for "mousey". My dad's mum also had jet black hair. Dad kept his dark hair, well what he had left of it, till his dying day.

It must have been quite a challenge, trying to keep three kids who didn't really do with each other, content on Holiday. I found a picture of me as a baby, with my brother and sister laughing and holding onto me as I sat astride a Black and White donkey outside the slots in Pendine. A coloured photo, so Mam and Dad must've bought a colour camera by then. I'd endlessly nag Mam for pennies for the slots every time we went on holidays. I also went through the same emotions each time. Excitement at going in, followed by the pleasure of winning and having to tell all who'd listen that I'd won. Those dirty one pences and big two pences never did come back out of there in my pocket as the disappointment at losing them all back to the machine, got me every time.

There aren't many pictures of me as a baby or as a young boy, to be honest. Remember, that I was the third born, and the excitement of photographing everything a baby did long gone from our family. On the other hand, the pictures of my sister, and to a lesser extent my brother, going through their everyday growing were much more numerous. My brother's reasoning for this was always the same, "It's because you were adopted! It always got the desired effect of feeling upset and a quarrel would then start. The picture I remember most, is of me on top of the piano in the parlour where I was born, in baby clothes that make me look like a girl in a smock. I've got a cocky smile in the picture, my hair in a side parting like an old man, but you should see the size of my head – like Nobby Styles' football!

Once, on a day trip down to Pendine sands, we came across a woman's handbag strewn across the road outside Carmarthen. The bag's content was everywhere. There were American dollars in the bag, all sorts of makeup and a hairbrush. It was quite obvious that there was something very wrong here, and by the time we'd reached the police station in Carmarthen, my mind was alive with thoughts about what I believed had happened. Who's bag was it? Had she been taken against her will? By the time we reached Pendine, and me and Dad were stood waist-deep in the sea, I was convinced that something very sinister had become of her. I imagined having to go back to the police station, to give a full report on how we'd found it. In reality, the police told Mammy that if no one claimed the bag within 30 days then she could have it and keep it. Mam was starting to regret even handing it in as it was an expensive Good brown leather bag and regretted it even more after those 30 days when she was told that the bag had been claimed without a word of thanks.

As a child, I was also brought up on some of the more gruesome stories of Pendine. They were all tragic, and each one ended with a fatality or two! The bus that lost control as it came down the hill, killing those on board, or Ronnie Harries who crept out of his bedroom window in his house in Pendine and then bludgeoned his aunt and uncle to death. He was the last man to be sentenced to death in Carmarthen or the tragic story of Babs which claimed the life of its driver Parry-Thomas. Each one is still very much in my memory to this day. I've always enjoyed a dramatic story, however gruesome.

If we weren't in Pendine, then we were in Tenby. Trostre's tinworks "stop fortnight" overlapped with the "miners fortnight" and we never holidayed at Porthcawl, as it would be full. Treco Bay would be jammed packed with holidaying miners from the valleys, before the development of holidays abroad. Apparently, they would go there in droves, and from the same street to get a bit of sun, too much beer and let themselves go for a week.

Living as I do far up in North Wales these days, one of the things that I miss most, is not being able to pop over to Tenby for the day. We'd go to Tenby every year, many times a year. We'd stay in Zion Gardens at the bottom of St John's Hill which was near to town. We did this for years, either in the flats or in one of the Holiday houses, or even one of the caravans. We'd look down our noses at the mass of Holidaymakers down Kiln Park because we were staying in luxury flats opposite John Beynon's lovely home. We were practically Tenby residents in our minds. We'd get the bottom flat, with its yellow stable door, while my dad's brother, his wife and family were in the flat upstairs. Dad was in his element being able to spend quality time with his brother Norman, his wife Sheila and the boys.

We'd go to burn at the beach every day, swim in the sea in our bathers, or build a wall with aunty Sheila to stop the tide from coming in. Building "the wall" was important to us all, and especially for Aunty Sheila, who loved seeing us do something physical as opposed to laying on the beach and burning to a crisp. I will be forever grateful to Aunty Sheila, who taught me how to float, in the sea in all those waves. I never did learn to swim, but I like to think that if I was ever in the sea, drowning, I'd be able to flip onto my back, put my ears under water and float to the safety of the shoreline.

When the weather didn't permit barbequing the body in the sun, we'd spend the day walking around the shops. Woolworths would always be open late and somehow would always have something that I'd desperately need to spend my Holiday money on. We bought a dingy one year, After days of nagging my mam. It was an orange and blue plastic Octopus lll, but we didn't get too much use out of it or much enjoyment either, as that same year there were plenty of stories of the sea claiming victims who'd been dragged out to sea, and drowning was a real dread of mine. Mam was always in charge of the finances and Dad was given weekly pocket money to spend on his favourite past time, horseracing. Mammy would insist that if we were in the sea, we couldn't go deeper than our waists, in case the sea would drag us out, out of our depth and we'd drown. Ever since, I've been frightened of going out of my depth, though I'd always prefer to "swim" in the sea than in a swimming pool.

If we were all on the beach, Mammy would never go into the water, for anything other than a paddle. Her shame about how she'd look in her bathers beating any fun in the sea every time. Her self-image hindering her from being herself. Poor Mam. Her family criticism over the years managing to delve deep into her very being. And us, through our ever-conscious feeling of embarrassment about our bodies, starting to do the same. Wearing a t-shirt into the sea and lying flat on a towel – life skills that a fat kid learns in order to hide from the truth that everyone else can see plain enough.

Daddy'd come into the sea. I'd always nag him to swing me around in the waves, however much I weighed and I'd enjoy chatting with him in the sea. Dad wasn't much of a swimmer either and though he'd try to dive in to swim under my legs, he'd never quite succeed. He'd dive in for what seemed like ages, and then come back up more or less in the same place as he went down, but we'd have a great time.

Our delight, as a fat family, was to eat Fecci's local ice cream. The only one who didn't follow the trend being my sister, who was always a different shape from the rest of us, and who kept herself slim and smart. It wasn't just that we'd always get two scoops of ice cream every time, but would also pay extra for fresh squirty cream on the top too. Looking back, I can just imagine what the holidaymakers of Tenby thought of us as we walked the streets of the town, in our shorts and pack a macs carrying our cones like the torch from the statue of liberty in our hands.

If we weren't eating oversized ice creams, we were eating fish and chips. Full of salt and vinegar, and eating them in the newspaper as we walked around the town, walking along the harbour or passing the lifeboat station, and up towards Albert the Good's statue in all his glory, despite the odd seagull markings.

In the evenings, we'd all meet up in the Evergreen Inn, right by where we'd be staying under the viaduct. We'd sit in the beer garden outside the pub. I'd get half of Strongbow shandy every time, and that shandy would be flat by the time we left, having just sipped it slowly to make it last and spent so long trying to stop the wasps from enjoying it. I'd enjoy sitting with Dad, listening to the adults chat, my brother showing off to my cousins and my sister seeing herself as too mature to spend time with us.

Once, when I was around nine years old, I found some friends to play with, who were staying in a caravan near us. I've little recollection of their names by now, but they were brother and sister and very friendly. While everyone enjoyed outside the Evergreen, my new friends decided to take me with them around Tenby Town. On the way around town, she decided that I was her new boyfriend, and we walked around hand in hand. We hadn't mentioned our little trip to my mam as she would never have let us go. We didn't notice how late it got either, but I do remember starting to think that I was going to get one hell of a row when I got back. I noticed in the Busy Bee cafe on the corner opposite the Post Office, that it was midnight, and I started to panic. I could get a row for nothing much really, so the row that was facing me now was going to be huge.

We tried to get back home without being seen, but before we reached the site, we saw that people were out looking for us. My brother found us and told me that Mammy was going to kill me when I got home. Of course, my brother was in his element. He was going to have all the credit for finding us, even though we were nearly back home when he caught up with us, but also how he'd love the row that I'd get, and he'd get to be on Mam's side once again.

We went through a stage of going to Butlins Barry Island too, long before Gavin and Stacey. "Jewells got talent" started with my sister competing in a talent competition, playing the piano. She didn't win that year, but the following year, it was my sister and brother together. My brother sang while my sister accompanied him on the piano. Mam and Dad must've been very brave to even consider putting the two together on one stage as they'd never been able to get on together. But despite all the odds, the tension and the glare of showbiz, it was indeed a winning combination, winning a place in the grand finale at the end of the season. It meant a free holiday for us and because we were celebrating their success we got to go into the outside pool late at night. They didn't win the final, but had had their taste of stardom!

Another time we went and took Dycu Bill, Dad's dad, with us. We went "full board" that time, and were constantly having to respond to the bells that came over the tannoy summoning us to food. I can still smell that canteen in my mind. A mixture of warm salads and spam with that grafted carrot tinge that I hated. We were made to sit in the same seats all week, with little choice of menu. Despite my ever-growing size, I was a fussy eater, and Dycu Bill must have lost the will to live the day he saw me eat the bacon rind yet leave the bacon on my plate. I don't remember a great amount about that week, but do remember Mam and Dad trying to get me to the "Beaver club" so that I'd meet other kids my age. I hated it! I couldn't settle to play with kids that I didn't know, especially when I knew that my family was elsewhere enjoying. Once was more than enough for me. The other kids all spoke English, and they were cheeky with the adults. I hadn't been brought up like that and it made me realise that I didn't belong in that world. I'd been brought up in Ysgol Dewi Sant and Bethel Chapel, and had been taught to respect my elders.

Dycu Bill used to go to his bed each afternoon for a "rest" while Mam complained to Dad that he was hard work to look after. I'm sure that Dycu must've found it hard having to live with this constantly feuding family all week. Bickering and nagging being a staple diet to our behaviour, and I'd imagine, on looking back, a surreal experience for my Dycu. Though he was offered to go again, Dycu refused any further holidays with this particular branch of the Jewell family. *Better to stay home*, he thought!

My brother's singing talents got us another family holiday in 1975, though we paid dearly for this one. He was competing in the boys solo ages 12–15 in the National Eisteddfod Bro Dwyfor, in Cricieth, and our first family outing outside of South Wales. We'd booked to camp in "Eisteddfa" outside Cricieth. Mam and Dad had misunderstood the name and had thought that this was the official camping site for the Eisteddfod. It was a lovely place, very pretty, but we didn't camp down there. Dad couldn't believe that they'd tried to con us with that name! We finally found the official campsite, and put up our "giant pearl blue ridge 6 berth tent" in the middle of all the small tents. Now this was our first time camping and our first time in any social Eisteddfod gathering. We felt slightly Superior due to the size of our tent, which stood proudly bigger and higher than the others around us. Granted, we didn't have a posh "Continental" tent with room to stand up, though we'd longed for one, but ours slept six and with a sewn in ground sheet, was watertight. We had never come across Eisteddfod camping during our competing at the Urdd, and were completely unaware of the drunken shenanigans that go on National Eisteddfod week.

The important thing about that week was that my brother was competing and we had to keep his white ironed shirt clean at all costs. Our fellow campers that first afternoon were friendly enough, though all seemed in their late teens or early twenties. There was certainly a buzz there, and we laughed and mimicked the north walian accents that we could hear from the "gogs" around us. Mam was on her stool in front of the tent, warming supper for us all on the primus stove, and the evening I remember was warm and pleasant. It was an early night for us all, as my brother had his preliminary competition at 8 the following morning. It was comfortable enough to begin with on our first ever night of camping but were awoken at around 2 in the morning by what I can only remember as a party going on outside. Raucous laughter, and car lights around us. It got worse from then on, as we started to hear cars racing each other on the field and without the pleasure of having Windows, we couldn't see what was happening. Every now and then, our tent zip would get opened, and a friendly over chatty drunk would try to say hello. Dad had had enough by now, my mam was worried about the lack of sleep that would affect my brother's voice, and a general feeling of panic engulfed our tent.

Dad got hold of a cricket bat in the end, and as our" visitors" unzipped our tent and poked their drunken heads in, Dad would whack them with a cricket bat! I've got to admit that I'm really surprised that Dad didn't kill anyone that night, but I'm sure that many had more than a boozy hangover headache in the morning because of him. My sister went to sleep in the relative safety of our Hillman Hunter, having realised at that moment that she had finally outgrown our family holiday adventures. By the second night, Mam and Dad having complained so much and so loudly about the night before, my brother not having secured a place on stage, and tempers more tense than usual, we were allowed to move to the BBC camping field no less. Of course, there was an abundance of touring caravans and Continental tents and we stuck out yet again. The "Beverley Hill Billies" were amongst the middle class BBC. We had a very warm welcome by our neighbours who genuinely seemed interested in our story of woe from the night before, and they must've silently laughed at these camping "virgins" who'd got it so wrong on their first time out!

I'd like to report that we'd slept better that second night, but the thunder and lightning kicked in on that second night, and the heavens opened. We were warned not to touch the tent as it would cause the rain to come in! The following morning, was the aftermath of that horrendous storm. The "Continental BBC" tents had been flooded out during the night, the caravans stuck in inches of mud but our "giant pearl ridge 6 berth" was none the worse for wear. That was enough to end our first experience of camping, and you'd have thought that we'd never want to see a field again. But we weren't put off, even after the cat and dog arguments in the back of the car the whole way home.

Believe it or not, my father must've forgiven the con that was "Eisteddfa", as we went back again to stay there the following year during the horrendous heat wave of the summer of 1976. My sister'd turned 16 by then and I'd imagine, glad of a bit of independence while we were out and about, the thought of earning her own money in Woolworths, Llanelli kept her going. The family of 5 "go camping" reduced to 4.

This time, the experience couldn't have been more different. The First night passed reasonably easily, though my brother did think that there were people talking outside the tent at night. The following morning, Mam was in her long-length red leather coat, on her stool, frying bacon. She'd woken us all as "Delyth would be starting work now as it's 9 o'clock. I remember thinking that it was unusually quiet for a morning, with our neighbours seemingly still asleep. Of course, it was Mam who'd misread the clock. It was 6 o'clock in the morning, and my sister was probably still in bed.

We saw some beautiful places around the area while we were there. We saw a man fall into the river outside Beddgelert which got us into fits of laughter. I loved Beddgelert, having been fully sucked in by the incredible story of that brave hound. We even managed some time swimming in the sea at Cricieth, though Dad got me out of there pronto, when he realised what the brown floating fish that I was describing to him actually were.

That second night, and after a full and busy day, we settled in for the night. But my brother started his nonsense again. There was "someone outside the tent" again. He could hear them making strange noises and he'd never sleep. With all the horrendous memories of that First experience, still very much alive in our thoughts, Dad dressed and went out to see. Reassured that it was only sheep, we finally settled down. The following morning my brother woke up in a sweat. It had been warm, but he was convinced that he'd been warmer than everyone. Dad went outside to see a sheep cwtching into my brother from the other side of the tent.

We had a great week up in North Wales. I was nine years old and had had my first taste of somewhere apart from South Wales and I loved the experience but "I'd never want to live there!" How strange life can turn out!

Chapter 4
Chapel Life – Bethel, Seaside

Mam tried her best to get us to go regularly to Chapel. Bethel Chapel was meant to be our Chapel down Seaside. Mam reckoned that we were Welsh Baptists. I was always afraid of Seaside because we'd been brought up on stories about how "rough" Seasiders were. Mam had always said that she could never live on the other side of Union Bridge or past the station gates!

We had our Sunday best clothes for Chapel and Sunday school that followed it. We only needed to go down the High street, turn right at Peter the shop, over Devil's Bridge then past the iron works to Chapel, but it seemed so different to us. Alien territory, and a world away from the comfort of our back garden and bank. Mam took me to Chapel as a young baby that First Christmas in 1966, the youngest baby ever recorded there at the time, and apparently, my name is still there on the wall in the vestibule as a reminder of one of Bethel's own. People reading it now must think that the Prime Minister himself had visited, probably after England won the World cup!

Chapel was always going to be a strain on us all. Not the Bible stories nor the hymn singing, but the fact that there was so much fuss made about what we should wear, and being on time to avoid the staring after hearing the click of the door if we walked in late. My brother always said that he passed his O level Scripture because he remembered his Chapel stories, and had never picked up a book to revise. I remember often having to stare at the back of some mothballed stinking mink stole, the Lilly of the Valley scent meaning to mask the pungent pong of those horrible moth balls. I'd constantly nag Mammy for jubes when things got too boring. David Jones was amazing on the organ, and I can still hear his incidental music prior to the Chapel starting, though we didn't hear it all the time! My fear would be very real during the sermon. I dreaded the preacher saying that it was time for the children to come to the pulpit and recite their learnt verses from the Bible. Mine was nearly always the same, "God is Love" – short and sweet and the old deacons used to comment loudly to themselves "very true".

Dad, of course, worshipped the peace he had while we were in Chapel. Dad was a churchgoer by design, and had attended Llanon Church as a choir boy and had even learnt to play the violin there at one stage, though in all my years of living with Dad, I never heard him play.

Thinking back, we had plenty of fun in Sunday school. We mixed with kids that we didn't know, who didn't speak Welsh, though everything we did was in Welsh. Kitty and Elsie Jones, two lovely old spinster sisters taught us tonic sol-fa and took no messing. We also did loads of colouring. Old fashioned pictures of stories from the Bible, but only if we listened to the story first! Bribery in the house of God and it worked every time! I was a well-behaved little boy, though I use the word little with caution. My brother, on the other hand, could be naughty and quite a handful and often I was embarrassed that he was giving us all a bad name in my mind.

Our Sunday school trips were always a family affair. Porthcawl or Barry Island beach for the day and everyone chatting and laughing throughout the day. I must have been very young at the time, but I can remember holding Llywela's mam tightly all day. Llywela was my sister's friend, who many years later died tragically in her car with her baby safe in the back of the car. We'd have fish and chips and ice cream on the seafront, and that old-fashioned respectable humour getting shared around with the chips by the women. There were men there too, all still decked out in their Sunday suits.

As we got older, I can remember my sister getting baptised. She was 16 years old and as a baptist, you were only baptised when you were old enough to consider becoming a fully blown member of the Chapel.

I'd describe the atmosphere as very tense on the morning of the baptism. My sister worried not about the decision she'd made to be baptised, but whether or not she'd look OK in her white baggy gown. Would it go see-through when it went wet? Would she be able to cope with being tipped backwards into the water?

Such profound questions before a baptism! I doubt that any of us considered how God was going to accept another member to his church that day. She was one of two, Bethan Thomas was the other, Aunty Betty's daughter and the two were friends.

Mam had secured us the best seats in the house for this event. We were all perched in the front seat of the gallery to the right of the pulpit and facing the action. Like spectators at a bull fight we were there in all our finery, to watch my sister getting baptised and receiving her golden ticket to heaven. The First hymn got Dad and then me in streams of tears, the pride I can still see in his face and the tears in his eyes. But as a young lad of around 10, at the time, my main concern was that the preacher was prone to talking very slowly, and I hoped that he didn't keep her underwater for too long. She didn't drown, but I'm afraid to say that the experience had taken its toll on her, and ended up damning us all on the way home.

But the Chapel had already started losing its appeal to us as a family, as we grew up. Well, Mam started it. She must have had a gut full of the false respectability of the Chapel after years of turning up only to be told that She like us all, was a sinner going straight to hell. Mam never had time to go on a Sunday evening, as she had "too much ironing" to do! Every time someone asked us where Mam was, our answer was always the same! "she's home ironing" Aunty Betty, our lunchtime lady at school, and a fellow member of our Chapel, started it by saying" Where's your mam then? Ironing is she?"

I remember that Aunty Betty used to look after me sometimes. "Don't tell her your history!" Was my mam's warning, but I was my dad's boy. The father, who could take over an hour to fetch a newspaper from down the road, and, "tell everyone our business". That lovely father who could chat with anyone. In fairness, Aunty Betty also had an amazing skill of getting any information she wanted out of you. A milky coffee and a sponge cake and I told her all my latest "news". I loved her company and chatted with her like, "jacky-bloody-nory" as my mam would say..

Life was changing for us too. We'd grown out of Sunday school and saying our learnt verse from the bible on a weekly basis, but still wanted to go sometimes in case we went to hell for not going and we hadn't been baptised either. When I was approaching my O-level exams, I started to go back to Chapel on a Sunday evening, to say sorry and to ask for forgiveness, not for my sins but for my lack of revision!

Chapter 5
Christmastime at Our House

Christmas was always a big deal in our house. The catalogue would come out, and the ticking and coding would begin on umpteen pages by the three of us. We had Grattan and the chance of having more presents if Mam and Dad could pay over twenty weeks. We'd ask for all the world's treasures, but content with what we were given come Christmas morning.

Things had been very different for Mam and her sister when they were young. Mam was born just before the start of the second world war in 1938, and during her childhood, she'd get a Christmas stocking that included good and bad things. Some sort of sick "trick or treat" stocking. As well as the special fruit and oranges, and toys there would be a turkey foot or a turkey's head. Mam used to say that Christmas always brought a mixed reaction from her and her sister as they never quite knew what to expect from Father Christmas.

Mam always stuffed the turkey at Christmas, with stale loaf of bread, chopped onions and thyme stuffing. She'd also cook it the afternoon before Christmas day so that we could all have a warm turkey and stuffing sandwich before going to bed. We'd all get offered an Advocaat and lemonade or a babycham at Christmas, and they were always served in our special cut glass goblets from the china cabinet as long as we "made it last". Mam had bought the goblets in Eddie Ryan's auction long before my time. I've never quite understood who this "Eddie Ryan" was, but he had apparently lived next door to us in the double-fronted house, and after his death, they auctioned off his stuff. Mam ended up buying the two cut glass goblets, a big black and gold victorian teapot and an old family bible for some reason.

The three-piece in the parlour would be cleared so that we could place our Christmas presents out for all who called to see. It was a Black leatherette suite with bobbly turquoise nylon Seating as was the fashion at the time. As the youngest, I was always given the sofa while my sister and brother had an armchair each. Our presents would remain in the parlour until new year's day. After that, they'd have to be gone upstairs and out of the way.

Our Christmas tree would always be in the parlour window, with Mam's warning not to touch the tree. It would normally be an artificial tree, and Mam was in charge of decorating it. God forbid anyone who touched it after it was up and ready to go. There was quite a bit of status that came with the effort put in by neighbours at Christmas. Those who didn't put the effort in were discussed behind their backs, and there was a thin line that could be crossed easily if tree lights were too "gaudy" or a tree was thought to be "over the top". It was a yearly struggle to keep within the social boundaries of the High street's good taste and decency. Decorating the tree was a big deal in our house, and my mam's O.C.D. came out with the trimmings each year. Fortunately or possibly, unfortunately, I've inherited this decorating obsession too, and my own children have learnt not to bother trying to help.

I liken decorating a tree to arranging flowers in a vase. There's a special knack to it. Symmetry and a balanced approach in order to gain perfection. See Mam was right when she called me an "odd ball"!

Up until the age of 6, the magic of Father Christmas was very much alive to me. I could never settle to bed on those nights before Christmas. I'd hear bells, see movement in the sky and generally be too excited to rest. We had a real chimney in the parlour too, and I knew that he used that chimney because I'd had a present off him early one year as I was home from school ill and on the settee in the middle room. It was before my birthday, I was fed up and all that I had to play with had got on my nerves.

Mam told me that she'd heard a noise in the parlour. I never worked out at the time, that she'd been hoovering all morning, and wouldn't have heard anything else. Mam hoovering while I lay on the settee was always of great comfort to me. Throughout my life, I've needed the noise to help me relax, and feel safe. To this day, I can't sleep without noise. Don't ask me how many hairdryers I've burnt out, and at the moment, I've got Alexa at my command with her "sleep sounds", in order to switch me off for the night. Apparently, I'm not the only one who hast his strange ritual, as Wayne Rooney does the same – and that's where the comparison with a sportsman ends.

I got up from the settee, and after much persuasion, went to the parlour to see to my astonishment that Father Christmas had been and left an easel and enough paint to entertain a little sick one. If ever proof were needed, this was it. Proof that Father Christmas existed and was looking down on us like a god in a red coat, and that the present I got early was given to me because I was a good boy. He really did exist and I had proof.

My Christmas dreams were prematurely shattered on Christmas day 1972, having only just turned 6. Father Christmas had come as expected, proof if proof was indeed needed of my Good behaviour throughout the year. I can still remember where I was, coming out of the parlour into the passageway, singing the praises of Father Christmas when my brother said in between pulls of laughter, that Father Christmas didn't exist at all and that I was stupid to believe in him. I argued that he'd never get any more presents if he went on saying things like that. He laughed louder as I cried harder in my temper, as my brother ran to the kitchen to tell everyone how silly I was to believe in Father Christmas. I was six years of age. Only six and the feeling of shame and ridicule overcame me as my mother confirmed what my brother had said and laughed at me for being so silly and getting upset. My brother, as was his pattern, was in his element for having managed to laugh at me and get Mam to agree with him.

Christmas was never the same after that, and letters to Father Christmas abruptly stopped. Looking back, it wasn't the brightest idea to tell me so young. I knew now, and couldn't blame Father Christmas if he ignored my Christmas list. It also made me realise that there were presents hidden around the house before Christmas. I'd go searching for them around the house, and my mam and dad had to find ever more sophisticated ways of hiding them. I found them one year in the bottom of the piano, and Managed to play with the Lone Ranger and his horse Silver for a couple of days before I was found out by my brother of course, and reported to Mammy as was the norm. "I'm telling Mammy," his battle cry.

One year, I was so desperate to open my presents that I woke at midnight. At two o clock I was so unable to go back to sleep that my mother told me to go downstairs myself to open mine. No one came downstairs with me, and I opened them alone. The guilt that I felt was overtaken by Mam's anger when she did get up. Apparently, I'd spoilt Christmas that year for everyone!

My sister worked hard at school, and her exams in the Girls Gram were always after Christmas. When my sister revised, she needed complete silence, unlike me. She could also learn vast chunks of text off by heart, and Dad would spend hours testing her on what she'd learnt. One Boxing day I remember that she insisted on silence while we protested as we couldn't play our new music.

I've always said that having a birthday so close to Christmas was a miserable thing. Having been brought up at a time when children were allowed to bring in their birthday cards, I could never do that as we'd always broken up for Christmas. In the same way, I'd have to look forward all year to my birthday which should've been special, but was always overshadowed by that baby's birthday in Bethlehem eight days later. And as a final moan, I remember that birthday presents always turned out to be something that "you were meant to have for Christmas but you can have now"!

Chapter 6
School Community and New Experiences

Capel Als nursery was my first experience of formal education. I remember very little about it, apart from a slide and a little girl with blonde hair that I used to play with. Oh yes, and trying to run away constantly. Capel Als was on a nasty bend at the bottom of Marble Hall Road, and the entrance to the vestry was on the side. My dependence on my mother was solid by the age of three. Arwel Morgan's father, Eddie Morgan was the one who'd bring me back each time, kicking and squealing. For years after, I remembered that event every time I saw him!

Ysgol Gymraeg Dewi Sant was my junior school. The First Welsh language school under local authority control, which opened in 1947. Where we lived, most of the other kids went to the local primary next door but we went to the Welsh school. Not only an ordinary Welsh school either, but Ysgol Dewi Sant no less.

I'd often considered what inspired my mam and dad to make the brave decision to put us into Welsh-medium education. Was it specifically the chance for Welsh-medium education, or possibly the chances that could come with being bilingual, or even the standard of the education? I asked Mam. Her answer was simple. "Dewi Sant was the nearest school at the time!"

Before I started going to school there, I'd go with Mam down the road to fetch the other two. The wall that we'd stand by on the street before the steps going down to the yard is still there. The Black stone is made out of industrial slag waste above the High red-bricked wall. I remember Heini's father, as a parent, a preacher and a real character playing hell with the mam's waiting as he pulled the zips of their dresses. There was nothing sinister in his actions, and the mams would giggle and feign offence at the attention he was giving them and everyone would be laughing and enjoying the nonsense.

We only needed to walk down the road to reach our school. We were at Dewi Sant and the English Copperworks School was next door to us. We'd share a canteen, though otherwise we'd be kept very much apart. Talk about creating a conscious split between the "Welshcakes", and the "welshnots". We shared the cook too and her name was Mrs Fry – honest. What's even more strange is that when the school moved up to Llannerch fields, our new cook was Mrs Philpott!

We'd always get a row if we were heard talking English, and the threat was always that we'd have to go next door to the English kids! We feared these English kids at Copperworks as if they were less fortunate than us, and would try hard to stick to the no English rule, in order to avoid getting beaten by "them" on the other side of the railings.

The older kids at Dewi Sant used to play bulldogs from one side of the tarmac yard to the other, and I remember that the toilets were outside and very unwelcome and would freeze solid every winter. We'd love to play "sticky sticky glue," but if we werefeeling unwell, we'd walk around with Aunty Betty, Mrs Price, or Mrs Thomas. Mrs Spufford was our cleaner and caretaker and worked hard to keep the school in check. She knew Mam, but would still shout at us if we got to school too early in the mornings. Her bark was much worse than her bite.

One of my earliest memories is of going to school for the first time and playing with the large farm board that was in the middle of the room. Mam took me in, and disappeared while I went to tend to the plastic animals on the farm.

Every day, I'd see some kids struggling to leave their mams, but I'd overcome that problem at nursery thanks to Eddie Morgan and apparently liked going to school. I remember feeling safe at school, enjoying the playhouse, liked singing and listening to stories being read to us. I remember meeting a little girl called Samantha in the yard on one of the first days. I ran back to Mammy and whispered to her, "Samantha Black arsehole!". Where that came from I'll never know, but with an older sister and brother, I always picked up sayings and rude words. Mam laughed at my comment but told me to be quiet, so I take it that she was used to the saying too. Till this day, I've no idea why.

After a year in the nursery with the lovely Mrs Smith, we moved up to Mrs Williams's class. Out of everything about her, what I remember most were her constant threats that any misbehaviour would result in a "couple of clatches". I knew that Mammy had been in the same class as Mrs Williams in the Grammar School, so made sure that I never experienced the threatened slaps.

I was a good boy in school. I enjoyed going when I could, but was always sickening for something. Till this day, I honestly say that I've never understood imperial or metric measurements as I was ill when they did that at school. When I moved up to North Wales at the age of 30, with my new young family, and went out to buy a Christmas tree, the garden Centre worker looked incredulously at me when I asked for a 20 foot tree for my house. I wanted a big tree for my bay window, but he thought that I was buying on behalf of the local council. Fair play to him, he was very polite and showed me a great tree that was just right for us. A seven-footer which took its place beautifully. Me and measurements have never got on, and I blame it on being ill at Dewi Sant.

"Best in bud" was the prize that I picked up one St David's day, by no one less than Llanelli's Lord Mayor in Parc Howard in front of the crachach of Llanelli's Society. But it's time that I confessed, that I was cheating! We'd all been given a daffodil bulb in school, to nurture and grow for St David's day to raise money for some cause or other. On the Thursday before the Saturday, John Morris Williams the headmaster was blowing a fuse on stage in assembly, as a warning to us all to make sure that there'd be a good representation from Dewi Sant at the Mansion house on Saturday. My bulb was still in my school bag, un-nurtured and un-grown. Luckily, daffs were late opening that particular year, and I was worried that taking one of the open daffs wouldn't be the same type as we were given. So I ended up with a daffodil in bud in a terracotta pot, straight from the garden. I won a prize. I've always carried the guilt of this deceit with me until now, but it was worth it. The headmaster's face on Monday morning was a pleasure to see. Lots of shaking hands on stage and the wrongfully earned thousand marks for the Yellow team.

Most of us will have a favourite teacher and maybe strange reasoning behind that choice too. In junior school, mine was Mrs Nicholas. I really loved being in her class. I can see her face in front of me now. An incredibly kind and nurturing woman, who spoke softly and if you disappointed her you really felt that you'd hurt her. She hardly ever rose her voice, unless to tell Mark Smith or Nicholas Michael off, but would always be ready with her cwtches if they were needed. My dependence on my mam had been well established before I started school, and having Mrs Nicholas (I never got to know her first name), in my life was a great blessing. She reassured me during a changing time for me and I've always appreciated her for that.

It's strange what you remember when you allow your mind to think back. I'd been ill again, and off for the week again. "There's no point you going back on a Friday!" Mam would say, and so I returned in full health on Monday morning to Mrs Davies's class. The first thing she asked me when I walked in was what had been wrong with me this time. I felt a real embarrassment, mixed with feeling upset that I was having to justify an illness yet again even though my mam had given me a note. "What's been wrong with you again this time then, Robert Jewell?" she asked. Was I going to say the truth or make something up? But I was fed up with her doubting my sickly absences so I told her the truth. "Diarrhoea miss!" Her face said it all and she never asked me again.

Being a pupil at Ysgol Dewi Sant carried with it a certain amount of status snobbery, apart from feeling that you were different from all the local kids. It made you proud to be able to speak Welsh. In an era of learning poems by heart, and when school assemblies represented singing well-known hymns, Dewi Sant was at the forefront of encouraging Welsh pride. The hymns and carols were the same as our Bethel hymns and carols – Miss Tomos a good clean living baptist from Bynea who taught Standard 4 in the room with the coal stove that she'd have to feed throughout the day. I was never taught in that room as we moved school site when I was in Standard 2, but that local Dewi Sant turned into a new modern Dewi Sant miles away, that we'd need a lift to get to every day.

We had great respect for the teacher at Dewi Sant. Their word was law, and on the whole, they were very fair. I might be wrong, but I don't think that either my sister or my brother had the same experience as me. They'd both failed the 11+; one with great disappointment and the other expected. The eleven plus had gone by the time I reached Form 4, but I like to think that I'd 'be passed, though we'll never know.

I really enjoyed learning my timetables in the quiet room with Mr Tomos, or Tommy tomato as he was known to the kids at the time. He was a very tall, thin, jovial man whose face would go as red as a tomato when he lost his temper. He had a wonderful big smile, and if you did your work then you had nothing to worry about. The work wasn't difficult for me and I never struggled and never got a smack from any teachers though many did. As a past teacher myself, I can't even imagine being given the right to physically hit a child, nor would I want that right, but those were different times. Smacking happened at regular intervals at school, and full-on public humiliation smacking with an out of control beetroot-red faced headmaster on stage in full assembly happened too.

There was a story that Mr Tomos would always tell my brother off when he was in his class, and my brother had come home complaining that the teacher was poking him on the head to make him work. Anything against his kids was like a red rag to a biul for Dad. Apparently, though not confirmed, he marched down the school, found Mr Tomos's class and threatened to come down and poke him on the head if he ever touched my brother again. It's just dawned on me that maybe Mr Tomos was so nice to me because of my father's threats, or maybe it was because I knew how to behave in class. I know from seeing my brother in Sunday school that naughtiness could flow in his blood sometimes!

Miss Tomos, (no relation to Mr Tomos by the way, and very much a Miss), the Standard 4 teacher was a stern character that you wouldn't mess with. She'd been a teacher at Dewi Sant since 1947 when it opened and taught in the old way! We studied "Scripture", every morning for an hour in Standard 4, and then everything else for the rest of the day. Miss Tomos had her "chronies" and neither my sister nor my brother fell into that category as they never seemed to impress her, but I had a feeling that she liked me. She'd sit behind her desk, preaching for the first hour of every day. Her whole demeanour from a bygone era. Her pearls and "two-piece" dress and jackets, and the naughtier amongst us noticing that she'd always sit legs apart with her bloomers on show. A slightly mortifying recollection for a teacher that was firm but fair. Apparently, she'd mellowed a lot by the time I reached Standard 4. She inspired me for a while, to keep going to Chapel on a Sunday evening, to note the preacher's sermon reference from the Bible. But only for the 200 marks for the Yellow House that I'd receive on a Monday morning. I never

ever thought of making it up and not going, though I'm sure That I could've done. Winning marks for the House was a big thing, and the winning House named every Friday in assembly. I was in the Yellow House and very keen to win marks for the team.

I knew that she liked me when it came to performing in the school musical. In our final year of junior school, it was our turn to put on a performance for the school and the parents. No modern high school musical type script for us! Miss Tomos chose an old poetic masterpiece called "Alun Mabon," from the 19th century by John Ceiriog Hughes which starts like this, "Roedd Alun Mabon yn ei ddydd, yn fachgen cryf a hoyw!", which roughly translates as, "Alun Mabon in his day, was a strong and gay boy". She gave me the main part. I don't think that she was consciously trying to out me at the time, but I do remember the giggling when we'd read that start. I had to memorise large chunks of poetry by heart, which I can recall to this day, but more than that, she wanted me to choose my love interest for the part of Menna Rhun from the girls in the class. These were more my friends than any would-be love interest, and though none of them wanted to be chosen, I remember choosing Menna Richards, who never quite forgave me for the shame of it.

Singing and performing were big in our school, and the musical action song was very popular. In a school like Dewi Sant, with so many parents keen to culturally "push", their kids, being a star in a musical show or nativity performance was a big deal. I still have so many Welsh language hymns and carols in my head, thanks to Ysgol Dewi Sant.

I tried to shine, starlike in the primary, enjoying the success of one of the narrators in the Christmas nativity show.

The Christmas nativity show was important to us in such a Christian school. We'd pray in the morning, before lunch and when it was time to go home. Heads bowed, eyes closed and hands together in prayer. Every year, the story of THE Birth was the same, with no place for the modern gimmicks of, "the sad Christmas tree!" or the "teddy that stole Christmas". Even the costumes were the same, and I got used to that large turquoise blue sequenced maxi dress though I'd be ridiculed every time for wearing it. I always imagined it to be one of Miss Tomos's cocktail dresses from her golden era.

My only disappointment as one of the narrators was that I didn't get to perform it from the beautiful ornate balcony of Siloah Chapel down Seaside, as we'd moved to Llannerch fields by then. The majesty of the balcony was replaced with a school stage, and apparently, the school had been too small by the time we got to it as the council hadn't been prepared for the surge in Welsh-medium education.

We'd learn the script off by heart so as not to let the teachers down on the night. There'd be an audience of proud parents, packed like a tin of red-faced, sweating sardines trying to get comfy in their small chairs with little leg room. I got to "narrate", for the last two years of my school life at Dewi Sant, and Miss Tomos led the way to equal opportunities, with her female Joseph in our final year. Delyth James was a tall girl, not like a man in any shape or form, but the role was important, and a wise and conscientious person was needed to lead Mair to the stable.

1977 was an important year for Ysgol Dewi Sant. The Queen's Silver Jubilee came to a very loyally royal Llanelli, who felt very privileged that the Queen and her husband were prepared to slum it and visit the peasants. We still have a cine film of the event. The town's school were all invited up to Park Howard, to watch her walk through the precious rose beds that no one else was ever allowed to walk on, and Llanelli Council wanted them to have a taste for the town. Two Welsh-medium schools were chosen to perform for the Royal party, namely Ysgol Dewi Sant and Ysgol Parc y Tywyn from Burry Port. The US and THEM of Welsh Medium Education continuing to alienate the general population.

There was great excitement with the parents and children – all that performing had paid dividends. A Royal Performance no less. If I remember correctly, only about half a dozen parents objected to having their children perform like serfs to the ruling oppressors, and us royalists incredulous at their stance at the time. Mammy said they were being "silly," and, "missing a chance!". A chance of what, I never could decide in the middle of all the excitement.

I wonder what Ysgol Dewi Sant would make of such an offer today?

We were to perform a musical action play, outdoors, on a setup stage placed right in front of the other schools. Proof if any was needed of the importance of the "welshies" over the rest. Ysgol Parc y Tywyn had it worse than us. They had to perform a typical rugby game, repeated as many times as it took until the royals got to them.

We presented an all-singing, all dancing act, and everyone involved had their time to shine in the front of the stage. Margaret Thomas, "the flower lady" (and only child of Mr Tomos, our teacher) was directly before me and Arwel Morgan, (the son of the Rev. Eddie Morgan who saved me from the road many years earlier). We were "the healthy rosy-cheeked butchers, who sold you meat…" thinking about it, we must have been depicting characters from Llanelli Indoor Market, and the butchers there were fat too, and we were certainly rosy-cheeked after dancing and singing for an hour in the summer heat while we waited for her to get to us.

As the Queen made her way slowly down the hill towards our stage, Margaret was there offering flowers to kids on the stage who weren't concentrating as "She" was coming; the headmaster, Mr John Morris Williams (a nice man but prone to explosive temper tantrums at times and feared by us all) standing to the side of the stage with Mrs Davies on the piano shouting at us to "sing out". As she reached the headmaster, it came the time for the fat butchers to shine in the sun. We sang on top of our voices, did all the moves that had been "drummed" into us, and we couldn't believe our luck. She was right in front of us. In case you're wondering, as Mam did, she wore deep pink lipstick and a light blue costume with a matching hat. I remember the headmaster shaking hands with her, and telling us all afterwards to our delight, that he'd never wash his hand again!

Mam got to meet the Duke too. He saw her with a bag full of sandwiches and pop, standing behind the barrier right in the front with my brother, waiting to raise the union jack. He walked over to where she was, and asked her what she had in her bag. Mam loved repeating this story and adored the Duke of Edinburgh forever more. "A lovely man," was her assessment, without further criticism. These days, I think that Mam would have had her bag checked prior to any contact with a Royal by MI5, in case she'd be carrying something more sinister.

By September 1978, the stardom had ended, and I was facing the same secondary school as my sister and brother, though it had been a Sec Mod when they went there. To the "new look" Comprehensive I went, having changed to its new status the year before. The remnants of the old 11+ failure system caused quite a bit of concern for us at times. I remember one boy, in his final year of school, whose duty was on a daily basis to go from class to class giving water to teachers' plants. The idea that everyone had a role to play in Society was a Good socialist idea and created a Good school community which I'm glad to say, survived with the change of school status.

I also realised that our fully blown Welshness that had been enforced at Dewi Sant was going to be ruined forever and that the bilingualism and Englishness that we encountered by meeting other schools was a step into life that was the real world. I became a little fish in a big pond, and my star had started to lose its sparkle!

Part 2
Family Influences

Chapter 7
Our Bynea Aunties on Mam's Side

In case you're wondering, Bynea is pronounced "bini yeah", and Mam had three maiden aunts who lived in Station Road, Bynea, and played a big part in my childhood and in my mother's childhood before me. They were Dycu Jack's sisters and they lived in the family home that had been built for them all in 1902.

Aunty Annie with her wonderful cologne smell was the eldest of the three. I can honestly say that she was the nicest person that I've ever met. A kind, witty and wonderful old lady. She, like her sisters, had always lived in the same house, and over the years she had collected feather mattresses for her bed, one upon the other. Mam remembers when she used to sleep with her as a young girl, and that it was as if she was sleeping on clouds. She always smelt nice. Eau de cologne was a firm favourite and all around her smelt exotically sweet. Aunty Annie had worked for years with her sister, Mary Hannah, in the iron factories handling and turning iron sheets. It was dirty and dangerous work, though as they got older they got out of there and Annie ended up as the top cook in Duport Steel works canteen. Apparently, her custard slices were legendary!

Aunty Annie was the cook in the house. Washing clothes on a Monday, baking on a Tuesday and eating fish on a Friday was the routine. If we were wise we'd manage to "drop in" to say hello just in time for a fresh loaf to take home. When I was little, though I'd always question the word "little", Aunty Annie used to make me a birthday cake. It was always a flat slab sponge cake covered in butter icing and with edible metal balls and hundreds and thousands on top. This was always a dream come true for this fat kid. Sometimes the icing would be coloured pink too due to her use of cochineal. If the outside looked lovely, the inside looked and tasted spectacular. I still don't know how she managed to make it a harlequin two colour inside but it was amazing!

Another treat that Aunty Annie had for us was her magical "bottom draw" full of chocolate bars. We'd have to wait patiently for the invite to follow her upstairs to her tiny bedroom, but would be awarded with some Fry's Cream or other such delicacies.

Aunty Lucy was the "lady" of the three. She'd been ill "since she was fourteen", and was told to keep indoors for her health's sake. Lucy May could look after herself well enough, especially as everyone else tended to her as well. She ruled her kingdom from the sanctity of their "middle room," where they lived. After saying this, she always quoted a certain Dr Sam who'd once said that if she kept doing as she did, she'd live until she was a hundred. He wasn't far off, as Lucy May lived until she was 89, having been cared for by others for most of her life.

In her final days, and sitting like the "queen mother" in her bed, when I'd come back from University I'd go to see her. She used her posh English with strangers and visitors, and as time went on she lost touch with who we were. I'd become very close to her in her final years, appreciating at last how wonderful hearing stories from another age were. She was hospitalised at Bryntirion Geriatric hospital, but she would have known it only as the old Workhouse and had she realised that then she would have been deeply ashamed of what had become of her. "Don't go too near her, she's smelling of pee'" was my mam's comment, but I ignored her and saw her for that final time before she died.

Lucy May was the one who wrote any correspondence from the home, continued to praise and quote Lloyd George "the great Liberal," and enjoyed arguing "Labour's politics" with my father when we called to see them. Aunty Lucy was also in charge of the beautiful fuschias and orchids in the small greenhouse, and no one was allowed in there, though we managed to "pop" those flowers now and again when she wasn't looking.

To complete the memory of the Bynea three, there was Aunty Mary Hannah. Aunty Mary was the outside worker. Quiet and hard-working, seldom complaining and always out smoking her compost pile, growing vegetables and weeding around the roses. Her work was never-ending and she had a weathered face to match. Aunty Mary had a sharp streak and if she was upset about something then we all knew. It would work up inside her until she exploded, but it was never aimed at us children. We'd laugh at the way she said certain things and enjoyed her kindness towards us.

The three were spinsters and had been brought up after the first World war when spare men were hard to come by. We only ever had one inkling of any sort of romantic possibility with them. We found a book when we were clearing out the home. There was an inscription in the book. It said, "To Lucy, Love Gomer X". "Love Gomer!" and an "X". I considered for many years what type of man Gomer may have been. The only thing that I knew for certain is that there never was an Uncle Gomer!

The other as yet an unmentioned member of the household was of course Jimmy. Or "good boy Jimmy" as he was always referred to by the aunties. Jimmy was a green and yellow budgie who lived in a small cage on the sideboard in the middle room. We'd be thoroughly entertained if we called after chapel on a Sunday evening to walk in and be greeted by the respectful chapel ladies calling after the Service for a cup of tea. They'd be in their chapel hats and their best frocks chatting away to the budgie. I remember particularly, a neighbour called Ethel Whitehouse, whose voice moved up a few octaves when she greeted the budgie whose respond by hitting his mirrored bell with his head.

The Bynea aunties were like the unofficial deacons of Tabernacle Baptist Chapel, Llwynhendy. Annie and Mary Hannah would walk over every Sunday evening and get a lift back from another chapel member. Sometimes, the preacher himself would call, and if Cecil Jenkins, Tabernacle was visiting, everything bar a red carpet was laid out before him.

Tabernacl, Llwynhendy was their Chapel, though their father had been First, treasurer of another Chapel down the road called Soar, and their parents and other family members had been buried in the graveyard there. "There was some quarrelling," was the only explanation that my mam ever gave me for the split, but when Mam and Dad got married, in Tabernacle they tied the knot, on a Tuesday. Apparently in 1958, getting married on a Tuesday was seen as classy.

They came from the remnants of the late Victorian age. You never praised your own children. Everyone else was praised as an example to us, but we were judged and criticised to our faces and we'd have to sit there on the sofa, taking it all with no answering back. They'd keep the praise they had for us to tell other people. We'd always have to hear about someone who was a "Scholar" at school, or a "good teacher," and our achievements are never seen as comparable at least to our faces. "You stick at school," we'd get told and you can be like Sid Abercynon, (their eldest brother) who'd been a headmaster at the Abercynon primary school many years ago, or Eira and Marian his daughters who'd done well down in Kent, and were "good teachers". Marian wasn't quite seen through the same pink-tinted spectacles as her sister Eira due to her bringing shame to the family by having an affair with her headmaster who left his wife to set up home with her. Marian and Keith were eventually sort of forgiven when they married. He brought Aunty Lucy some beautiful orchids for her greenhouse.

But of all the lovely memories that I have of my Bynea aunties, the best I have is of the small glass of very sweet homemade wine that we'd get to taste occasionally when we called. Dependent on the season, there was either elderberry or elderflower wine. Though they'd always claim to have never touched a drop of alcohol in their lives, the warm fuzzy feeling I experienced many times sitting in the car on the way home from there, was proof of its potency.

Chapter 8
Myngu Susan and Dycu Jack
Peggy and Jack on Mam's Side

Peggy and Jack were Mammy's mam and dad – big characters in Llwynhendy Road opposite Noel the garage. They lived in an old small terraced house that had housed a large family at some point in a time long before I can remember. An overwhelming smell of TCP everywhere, and Edwin who looked like a tramp living next door. The Llwynhendy house had an odd shape to it. I'd say that it was a two up two down house, apart from the fact that Myngu had a scullery the other side of the stairs, and above that room was Edwin next door's bathroom. I was always terrified of seeing Edwin next door, though he never did me any harm. I remember Myngu telling us that Edwin was nearly blind, and lived in poverty. He could hear but never see the rats in his house, and one of them had bitten off a piece of his ear while he slept. These rats were also resident in the large zinc wood storage sheds behind the houses. There was a right of way going through the house in Llwynhendy Road too, though we seldom saw anyone pass by the living room window.

As kids, we knew Myngu as Myngu Susan, in order to distinguish her from my father's mother in Lakefield Road that we called Myngu Norman. In this age, there could well be a Myngu called Norman, but ours was called Myngu Norman because my father's younger brother Norman was still living at home when my sister was born. So Myngu Susan got her name, as my cousin Susan lived with them when she was young.

I think it would be fair to say, that Dad was never their biggest fan!

Myngu Susan and Dycu Jack loved a bargain and loved a good route around a jumble sale. They'd always see a bargain in everything that anyone else didn't want. I have to confess, that I inherited this particular gene from the pool, and love a good rummage and I often wonder whether eBay would cease to trade if I stopped buying off them. I once experienced Myngu Susan in full battle mode when she took me to a jumble sale in the Parish Hall in Llanelli. We were there way before two, standing First in line in front of the door. Two o clock came and went, and Myngu became inpatient. She rapped the door with her entrance fee coin, shouting to the would be stall holders on the other side. "Come on, what's the matter with you, it's after two?" As if the bargains were going to disappear if they opened up late.

Myngu Susan could be very sharp if she wanted to be and she clashed hard and often with Aunty Mary Hannah, as they were cut from the same cloth. Often we'd get a tongue lashing off her, and Mam would say that she'd been like that with her as a child too. Myngu was one of eight siblings, I think, with a no-nonsense father who didn't spare the rod. In a large family of boys and girls, having a sharp tongue was an advantage I'm sure. We'd walk into the living room where she always sat and we'd get almost instant criticism. "Have you brushed your teeth today," or, "When did you last wash your hair, it's looking greasy". Myngu was famous for walking into a chemist and noticing a smiling shop assistant, approaching her and asking her which toothpaste she used. Or "what shampoo do you use?" before coming home ready to advise us the next time we called.

I can still see Myngu now in my mind, sitting in her low chair with her back to the breath-taking views of the Gower coast from her Picture window. Her square table would be half full of different vitamin tablet pots, that she'd read in one of her magazines would be good for her. Her right arm would be under the table holding a fag that always seemed on the go. Preaching about the benefits of vitamins while smoking like a steam train. In her last years, she worried more and more about the cost of heating and would sit by the fire with only the pilot light on in the gas fire. Fearful of keeping warm in case it costs too much.

Quarrelling in any family is terrible, but when you have big characters quarrelling, it turns bonkers for everyone. That's how it was for myngu Susan and the aunties from Bynea. I have literally no idea why the argument started in the first place. I have no idea how much credence I can give to the story that the Bynea family tried all they could to stop Peggy from marrying their dear little brother, but there was very little sign of a united front in the wedding pictures that we'd seen. Jack and Peggy married, and Mam was the first born to them with another daughter arriving six years later. The aunties took a lot of interest in Mam as she was Jack's first born, and they adored their little brother and managed to fill her head with judgement and self-doubt for the rest of her life.

Mam would go to Chapel with her aunties from Bynea. The aunties would encourage her to learn a new piece from the Bible each time, but if she didn't she'd have to rely on a part of the Scripture from Paul's letter to the Romans, which was in ceramic on the front of a house in Station Road, Bynea and in Welsh, roughly translated as "if you confess with your mouth that Jesus is Lord and believe in your heart that God raised him from the dead, you will be saved! The quarrelling lasted many years. We'd visit the aunties to hear nasty stories about Peggy, and then call in Peggy's on the way home to hear nasty stories about the aunties in Bynea. Dycu Jack flitted comfortably between both, seemingly oblivious to the hatred between the two waring parts of his life. He was the "golden boy" to his adoring sisters and "John" when Myngu shouted at him from the house to the old carriage train and sheds where he homed his budgies and canaries and was normally to be found.

Jack was the youngest, of all the Bynea family children. Tall and handsome in his younger days, with a mane of red wavy hair, like others in the family. I'd say he'd been spoilt as a child, and as the last of the offspring would have had it much easier than those before him. He always drove a three-wheeler, Robin Reliant, on a motorbike licence. He never passed his test to drive a car, and never took that step from three to four wheels. This fact may well have saved his life in time.

The stories about Jack and his three-Wheeler were legendary in our family. I remember when Myngu used to come in the car with us. She'd make a large grunting heaving noise ever time my father turned a corner as if she was about to be sick and used to grab the corner of the driver's seat and pull it towards her, much to my father's annoyance. She'd also repeat "o na beth mowr", which roughly translated means "oh there's a thing". To us kids, this was hysterically funny, but it used to really wind my father up.

I believe that her issue with travelling in the car started when Jack took her and Susan my cousin as a young child, to Tenby in the three-wheeler. They'd packed the car to the top with Susan perched towards the roof on a mound of sleeping bags. Jack was driving and Peggy in the passenger seat navigating their way. Apparently, Jack tipped the car over on a roundabout outside New Hedges, outside Tenby. Firemen managed to cut Susan out of the back. Shaken and very stirred but unharmed, Peggy vowed never to go in the car with him again and she kept to her word.

If Peggy and Jack wanted to go into town, Myngu'd go on the bus and meet Jack there as he'd drive in. They followed the same pattern on the way home too.

Once, After Peggy'd died, Jack drove down to Bynea to get chips for tea. Having bought the chips he got back into his car. He turned the key in the ignition and noticed a blue flame come from the dash. He put out the flame with a cloth from the car and tried to start the car up again. The car Engine blew up, and Jack managed to escape from the car to the safety of the pavement where he proceeded to eat his chips while the fire brigade put out the car fire. In this lucky escape, the one thing that upset Jack most was that the woman who'd had his car burning outside her house made an insurance claim against him for damaging and melting her uPVC Windows.

Another time, Jack was in his new three-wheeler following a successful Insurance payout on the burnt-out car. He was very proud of this new car and on its virgin voyage, drove it from the garage towards town. "This is the only blue one of its kind in South Wales," was his boast. To be honest, he was the only man that I knew of in South Wales who even owned one.

At a ripe old age, Dycu Jack continued to drive, despite the fact that he wasn't always safe on the road. He was a large well-built man, and the car would drop to one side when he got in it. These particular cars had never been famous for their safety features either, and tipping over was quite a regular occurrence for them.

On the first trip out in this brand new, special blue car, Jack was driving down the road towards Pemberton lights. He could see that there was a row of traffic in front of him, so he went to break. Unfortunately, the pedals on this new one were slightly different from his previous car and instead of braking, he plunged forward on the accelerator. To avoid an almost guaranteed collision, he opted for his best chance of Survival and turned the car leftwards and onto the empty pavement where he should've stopped. Unfortunately, he carried on down the pavement, down past the hair salon and straight into a lorry that was parked and tarring the road by the lights. The front central wheel saved Jack's life that afternoon. He avoided being another statistic and also avoided the same grisly end as Jane Mansfield. When Jack was finally cut out of the car, he was offered a cuppa by a well-meaning woman living nearby. Jack's main comment on the whole episode was to complain that the tea the woman had given her was "bloody cold!"

When I was teaching at Ysgol Tryfan in Bangor, at the start of the new millennium, I used to tell some of my classes Dycu Jack's car stories. They'd laugh though never fully believe me. If you're reading this Guto Rhys, and the others in the class, they were all perfectly true from my recollection.

Dycu Jack's "official", delight after retiring from Duport Steelworks was breeding canaries and budgies. A "Best in Show" rosette was a big deal to Dycu, and the competition often took him away from home. He also enjoyed growing his own vegetables, especially potatoes and carrots, though I do remember being amazed at the strange stick-like green things that he also grew, which turned out to be sprouts.

Jack also liked to try to change the natural order of wildlife. He'd put up a trap-cage at the bottom of his garden with a red bullfinch in it to try and attract other wild birds. He'd then try and breed these wild birds with his canaries to try and create "mules," as he called them. These were nearly always kept in the old carriage train. A completely illegal action, and one which was alien to the rest of us. To try to get us on board with his illegal breeding programme, he once gave me a caught bullfinch. He was a beautiful deep red one and brought it to me in a cage. I even named him, Bartholomeus, after my Standard 4 Bible studies though I knew deep down that it was wrong. When Dad saw it, sitting there, a world away from its natural life, he asked me if I thought it would be better left to go free. We did just that, though I'm not sure that leaving it out miles away from where it was caught would've been a good thing in the long run.

Dycu Jack was in my eyes, a bit of an Arthur Daley in reality, searching for bargains and wheeling and dealing. I remember when he emptied his family home in Bynea when Lucy May died. He sold whatever he could from there. Beautiful old pottery and wonderful old antiques all went the same way to a fellow artful dodger who I think would have seen him coming. He used the proceeds of the sale of his respected family's treasures to get himself a huge television that took over the living room. He had his favourites. His daughters adored him, as did my cousin Susan, but I was never a big fan and tended to stick to my father's side of the family.

Dad would always laugh that Jack was famous for his "bird watching on the Gower". He'd drive over to the Gower in his three-wheeler for hours in the Summer, leaving his wife sitting in the house. I never quite understood the reference or the negative effect it always had on Mammy when Daddy mentioned it!

Peggy was never accepted in the Bynea family home. She didn't look for their acceptance either. The only time that I can remember seeing Peggy in the middle room in Bynea, was during Aunty Mary Hannah's funeral. I can still see Peggy walking towards Lucy, reach her hand across the table and shake her hand. Lucy reigning supreme on her chair as usual, accepted her condolences, though her whole body shook after the encounter.

Quarrelling within a family is always a terrible thing, and it's still happening in the Llanelli family to this day. Some like my Myngu Susan, enjoying the excitement of a good argument and hatred much more than others, and Mam even in her old age enjoying, in the thick of it all, though protesting its expected devastation.

Dad quarrelled with Myngu Susan when I was young. She'd been overly critical as she was prone to do, and Dad's "top lip" had been getting higher and higher. Apparently, it was a "Jewell" trait according to Mam. My dad had a long fuse, but once it blew there was no turning back. Peggy'd said something about raising children, and Dad had answered that he was doing a better job of it than she'd ever done. And that was it! Out we marched from the house in Llwynhendy to the car, and we didn't go back for years. I remember as a child, seeing Myngu in the town outside Mcfisheries. She put her head down and ignored me. I was a young boy, and hadn't done anything to her. We didn't speak to her for ages, though we'd often see Dycu Jack in Bynea when we called. If we didn't talk to Peggy, then we also didn't talk to Aunty Ann, who'd taken her side against us. You see, sides again.

This ridiculous quarrelling went on for far too long, and the start of any reconciliation only began while Aunty Annie was on her death bed in the old Llanelli hospital. At 79, she lay there with a stomach so bloated that you'd have sworn that she was heavily pregnant. Her wish before heading for explorative surgery, was to see Mammy and Aunty Ann speaking again.

She got her wish and they became friends again before she went down to the theatre, but she never came back. That lovely mild-mannered, kind and sweet old lady, who'd never smoked in her life was riddled with cancer and they opened her up only to close her again. She never survived the anaesthetic and we felt a great loss from losing her.

After the three sisters had died, and a bit of the Edwardian social and moral life of Bynea had gone forever, Dycu had the task of clearing the house. We went over to see Myngu at Llwynhendy. She was sitting there as usual, in her favourite chair, a table of vitamins by her side and a single line of smoke coming from underneath. By now she was nearly blind, but when she opened her mouth to smile, she did so with easily recognisable teeth. But they weren't Peggy's teeth at all and it wasn't Peggy's smile. Her smile and her teeth belonged to Aunty Annie. Recycling at its most macabre!

Myngu could be very funny, and extremely sharp and witty at times, especially when she was repeating a story, but she was no traffic warden on the busy Llwynhendy Road outside her house. Dad would need to park against the flow of traffic when we visited, and of course, have to cross the traffic to get out too. Each time we left, Myngu would insist on trying to guide Dad from her front doorstep. "Go on Elwyn!" she'd shout, while Dad would damn her for even trying as," that bloody woman can't even see the traffic!"

The last time I saw Peggy, was when she was in Prince Philip Hospital, on Llanelli. She was completely blind by then and knew people only by their voice. Typically, I'd lost my voice and I wasn't there very long as she didn't recognise me and couldn't hear me talking. I took my then-fiance Mari to see Dycu Jack in his last days in hospital too. He'd been having small heart attacks for a while but continued to climb apple trees as a big heavy 85-year-old living alone. Mari was amazed to see the size of his head too! "A pretty girl", was his comment, and the "watching birds on the Gower" instantly came to mind.

After emptying out the house at Llwynhendy Road, I took my new wife to see the house one last time. The old smell of TCP remained as pungent as ever, and Mari was petrified in case a rat would jump out of nowhere and bite off her ear!

Chapter 9
Jinny and Dai Glynneath on Mam's Side

Almost every other Sunday, we'd go over to see Aunty Jinny and Uncle Dai in Glynneath. Well, it was actually in a village called Cwmgwrach, but I was always frightened of that name when I was young. The car would always be full, between Dad driving, me and Mam in the front seat and my sister and brother one each side of either Aunty Annie or Aunty Mary who'd sit in the middle. There was no concern about seat belts or what would happen in an accident!

Officially, Aunty Jinny was the youngest sister of the aunties from Bynea, and very near Dycu Jack's age. That's what we held to be true for many years, though there had been some whispers now and again about Jinny's father's family down the Hendre. Very recently, (as I get old and have started searching my ancestry), I've come to understand that Jinny wasn't Jack's sister at all, but his older sister, Lizzie Ann's illegitimate offspring. Jinny is mentioned in the 1911 census as "granddaughter" to the old John Thomas and his wife. Mam's side of the family has mostly lived to a ripe old age, and as I write, Mam's living her 81st year. Mam never met her Aunty Lizzie Ann. She died a spinster in her early 50s, who'd been kept in the house to work, following on from her very public "shaming". It was never mentioned in the house in Bynea, in front of us, but apparently, there had been an "unfortunate" encounter with the coal man in the coal hut at the back of the house and nine months later Jinny arrived. This would have been such a disgrace for the God-fearing, Christian worshipping family, whose reputation as a high moral and equally high status was so important to them.

This hadn't been the first disgrace to affect the Bynea family either. Back in the midst of time, there's talk of another Aunt Lucy, who was related to the old John Thomas. I think she might have been an Aunt of his and was very respectable within her society. I've got her Portrait in my garage somewhere, showing an un-smiling woman with long, flowing locks of auburn hair which would give Shân Cothi the famous Welsh singer a run for her money. She apparently lived near Loughor, and having returned from chapel one Sunday morning, noticed that her front windows weren't as clean as they should be.

She'd have a fit if she saw our windows or most people's these days. She quickly tried to clean her upstairs Windows by hanging out of the bottom and wiping them down just as the Preacher made his way up the road. In her panic apparently, from what I remember of the story at Bynea, she lost her grip as she panicked to try and get in out of the way. Working on a Sunday was, after all, forbidden. She lost her footing and fell from the upstairs window to the road below and died in front of the preacher. She paid the ultimate price for working on the Sabboth, her respectfulness and her vanity causing her downfall.

Think how much our world has changed. Me and my husband, my ex-wife and her new husband, recently took our three daughters to celebrate an 18th birthday in Liverpool. We all stayed under the same roof for the night without any questions or concerns.

Dai and Jinny lived far enough from her family. I'm not sure of this, but I think that Jinny may have moved away from the highly tiresome, moral virtue of the Bynea home, to start a new life in Cwmgwrach?

The truth is, that Aunty Jinny didn't have the nicest of lives, and I'm not sure whether she ever got to hide away from her mam's shame. She was a lovely woman with us, and would often give us "ten pence to go and buy yourselves an ice cream each", in the Billiard Hall in the Centre of Cwmgwrach. Mam would always need to contribute towards it, as Aunty Jinny hadn't been out of the house in 20 years, and had no idea of the worth of the money. I can still remember the taste of the Tutti Fruity.

Dai was from the community where he lived. Born and raised locally, and enjoyed a pint or three. Mam would repeat stories from when she was young, and Aunty Jinny and her would follow him home from the pub in the forest, laughing at him as he sang to himself and strayed from one side of the track to the other. He was very much an emotional drunk, but a drunk who frightened Mam. He'd come home crying and promise never to drink again until the next time. However funny it was, the experience of seeing Dai Morris drunk and out of control left its mark on Mam. Mam has never tolerated drunk people in her company, and Dad was never allowed more than three pints.

They never had any children, and Dai couldn't tolerate his own family either, though they lived in the same small village. He'd walk past them and swear about them, calling them all names. Jinny was the boss without a doubt, and she was always glad to see us when we came to see them. She'd spend most of the time cursing Dai with Mam, while we played shop in the pantry. Jinny had tins of peaches in that pantry that were from the war years. My dad's dread was always that she'd open some for us for tea with ideal milk as she often did. We'd play in that pantry for hours, amazed at what she had kept for so many years.

Alan was their lodger, and Jinny adored him. I suppose that he was a welcome change from Dai, and much wiser. Alan was a lumberjack, working weekdays in the forest behind Dai and Jinny's house, and returning home normally on a weekend but not always.

At the start of Jinny's long and drawn-out illness with cancer, in her early sixties, Annie and Mary would take turns in staying over for weeks at a time to look after her. Dai's welcome was lukewarm at best. They'd have to do everything for him, as he was a man who'd never had to do anything for himself. He saw them there as interfering. Dai was a weak man, and he continued to cry or himself and the mess that he'd made for himself.

When Jinny finally went to the old red hospital at Neath, dying of cancer, she'd hallucinate and have nightmares as her illness took over her life. The doctors suggested that could be the effect of all the medication, but her fear was the same each time. In her illness and her weakness, she'd imagine that she was seeing Peggy entering the ward from the far end, and walking towards her. Jinny was so frightened of her and was convinced that Peggy was there to kill her. Jinny, like her older "sisters", had argued with Peggy many many years ago, and Jack as always was caught in the middle and quite happy to be there, having the best of both worlds.

After Jinny's death, we'd still go and visit Dai at his home. By now, he had made up with his brother-in-law, Rex, and Dai and Rex would often watch television while drinking pints of sherry when we'd call at ten in the morning and there was very little welcome. The aunties had continued to look after him though he used them as unpaid help really. They did all his washing and his cooking and cleaning while he sunk ever faster into alcoholism with his new drinking partner. Mam wrote Dai a letter following our last ever visit there. The content was honest though not quite as subtle as it could've been. In her best English, she noted his weaknesses, his drinking and his lack of respect towards the aunties. "Jinny must be turning in her grave," was one line that I remember vividly, and noted how he'd used his in-laws. She finished her letter with this line, "You will not use me like you once used the Thomases."

We never saw Dai again, and he had a massive stroke not long afterwards, leaving all his worldly possessions to his sister and brother-in-law. More interestingly, though he had always promised that he'd "look after" Mam after he was gone, the will he left had been written months before any "falling out". As I said, Dai was a weak man!

One of the most horrible recollections that I have, is going to Aunty Mary's funeral in the cemetery in Tabernacle, Llwynhendy. Aunty Mary Hannah was buried in the same grave as Aunty Jinny, who had finally come home to be buried, the shame of her birth having finally been buried with her. The grave had been originally prepared for Dai and Jinny, but Dai's remains never made it back to Llwynhendy, though he'd spent a small fortune on a grave with concrete walls to keep Jinny's coffin dry. Maybe he was terrified of what she'd say if she saw him again after all that had happened. When they opened the grave on Aunty Mary's funeral day, we all saw that Jinny's coffin was floating on the top of a grave that was filled with water. But worse than that was to come. When they lowered Mary Hannah on top of her, there was a big splash, as the excess water rushed over the sides.

Chapter 10
Myngu Norman and Dycu Bill – Winnie and Bill – on Dad's side

Winnie and Bill were Dad's mam and dad. From them, we had the unusual surname, Jewell. Dad was one of four boys born to a couple who were obviously full of love for each other.

Rachel Winnifred Evans was from Llanelli, and her family came from West Wales, namely St Clears and Laugharne. Her father Gwilym died the January before I was born in 1966. He was a deacon in Caersalem Chapel, Tyisha, and liked to think of himself as a bit of a poet. He wrote under the bardic name of Gwilym Coran, though I've yet to find anything that he ever wrote in print. In his final years, Gwilym Coran would be pampered by his daughter Winnie. He was famous for asking for half a cup of tea or for leaving three peas uneaten on his plate.

In all honesty, I don't have many memories of Myngu Norman. She died when I was two and a half years old, but do remember her looking after me once while my mother went to town. It didn't happen often so I wasn't used to it but I remember that she did manage to quieten me down by showing me a salt and pepper set of a boy and a girl together.

One nodded yes and one nodded no and they fascinated me. I've still got them as cherished possessions of a time long passed. I also do recall having a coffee with her. Ideal milk and camp coffee. Delicious at the time but much too sweet for me now.

Dycu Bill, or to give you his real name, William Henry Jewell, originally came from Bideford in Devon. The Jewell surname quite common in those parts. Dycu Bill talked with a sort of "Scampy fries" accent as we'd call it after the television advert, and he was also one of four brothers. The family came over from North Devon on the boat across the Bristol channel and settled in the area around Llanelli. Dycu would've been about 13 years old and set out to look for work like his father in the mines. Life in the coal mines was hard at that time, and he'd had to stop working in his early 40s due to having silicosis.

They'd have had to learn Welsh to settle in Llanelli at the time, and I remember Dycu always able to talk Llanelli Welsh, though he'd never have managed to write it down. His English accent was always very different from ours.

With the Great Depression, hitting us hard in Wales like everywhere else in the 1920s, and Bill having met Winnie, he decided to emigrate to Canada to look for work in the coal mines out there.

I can only imagine the conversations that they must have had between themselves. Myngu worked in a shop in New Dock Road, and Bill pleaded with her to go out to Canada and start a new and better life with him so far away. I can also imagine how concerned her mam and dad must have been, from seeing this Englishman trying to steal their daughter who had'nt been half well after her scarlet fever as a child. She was also very fond of her family and held them in great esteem.

Bill took the plunge and made it all the way over to Alberta, to the middle of the tough and inhospitable terrain of the Rockies, to a place called Hillcrest. He managed to get work there and secured a place to live. He sent money over to Winnie in the hope that she'd follow him over there.

Winnie did indeed follow Bill, and they met in Calgary, after a fortnight's journey on board a ship. Her possessions were all put into one large metal chest. Bill was far from wealthy, and in order to meet her, had had to catch numerous trains before running out of money and did the last part of his journey by foot in order to meet her.

As he met her as she came off the ship, he asked her to marry him there and then. Aunty Sheila, Uncle Norman's wife, recently shared with me Winnie's thoughts at the time. She shared with Sheila, that having gone so far to be with him, she'd have been crazy to refuse him and have to go back on the next boat home!

It was late afternoon, and the night was falling, so they found a Welsh Baptist Chapel in Calgary, The place was closed, but they knocked on the preacher's house door, and asked if he'd marry them. The only witness to this marriage was the preacher's daughter, and after the Service, they went on their way to start a new life in the Hillcrest mountains.

Life was hard for them there, and my Uncle Ken, Dad's elder brother was born there. If life had been tough for two, it was even tougher for three, and after facing the reality that prospects were bleak, they took the decision to come back home to Llanelli. There were only 18 months between Ken and Dad, and Dad was born in Fron Terrace, Llanelli in March

1932. Winnie and Bill ended up living with her family after arriving back from Canada, penniless and having seen the harsh reality of being so far from home in such a barren place.

The couple had another two boys after Dad. Byron and then Norman. The young Jewell family, by now, were living in rented accommodation in the Plas, Llannon outside Llanelli. Byron the newborn apparently developed a reaction to some medical injection he'd received and died on Boxing day as a young baby. I can only imagine the sadness for this young family, who were poor financially, but rich in care and love for each other. Byron's grave stands proud in Llannon Church cemetery, and Dad's ashes went there to join him in 2009. The simple White wooden cross, which was such a treasured part of my childhood, was replaced by a lovely granite grave stone which bears the name of Byron and my dad, with room at the bottom for Mam's name when she dies. Their children were everything to Bill and Winnie, and when Norman arrived in 1938, their family was complete and they were always very proud of them.

Dad was named after Myngu's brother, Elwyn, who'd died at the age of 14 after being kicked by a horse. Closeness and family were very important to them. Myngu would go to Box Cemetery in Penallt, Llanelli for the day, and take flowers and a bottle of water, to clean up the family graves, weed around them and have a cup of tea and a few sandwiches from the picnic that she'd prepared. She'd enjoy looking around other people's graves too, something that I still enjoy doing if given the chance. Myngu'd love it, and Mam still has a picture of Myngu in her smart clothes, standing proudly by the family grave.

Bill moved with his young family from place to place depending on his work, and Dad used to tell me stories of when he lived in the old stables of Middleton Hall where the gift shop of the Botanical Gardens is now. Dad remembering walking to school on the winding country road with his two brothers to Llanarthne School, and myngu having to pay a local woman to feed her children every school day at lunchtime in the absence of school dinners at the time. They were "taught" by an old soldier from the first world war who didn't spare the rod but really spared them of any meaningful education. The boys were close to each other and that's how Ken, Elwyn and Norman remained for the rest of their lives.

Dad Also remembers Ken hitting another lad who'd try to pick on Dad. What Ken missed out on in height he made up for in his ability to support himself and those close to him. Ken had a temper, and his top lip would twitch as a fair warning prior to any conflict.

My father's memories of living in the stables of Middleton Hall used to frighten me as a child. There was a butcher in the corner of the stables opposite them, and if any of the workers found a snake in the overgrown walled gardens, they'd hang them dead from the trees' branches. Dad had nightmares for years after having run into some hanging snakes on a tree as a child. As long as I can remember, if Dad saw a snake on the television the inevitable nightmare would happen, and he'd be on his feet from bed in his sleep, fighting against them in the darkness of the landing.

Everyone knew the Jewell boys, and they like us were remembered by their community because of their surname.

Myngu and Dycu moved to Lakefield Road, in the older years after many years in Dilwyn Street, a stone's throw from

Dad's birthplace at Fron Terrace, Tyisha. By then Myngu was suffering with her heart and was meant to take things easier.

Myngu was one hell of a character. A genuinely mild-mannered exterior hid a steely determination. Full of fun and kindness she took care of everyone and was wonderfully bonkers at times. She'd read fortunes from tea leaves, and was extremely superstitious. She thought that people born in May were unlucky for the rest of us "the old cats of May". A broken mirror would mean seven years of bad luck and walking under a ladder equally worrying. If she spilt salt, she'd need to throw a pinch over each shoulder to blind the devil, and strangely enough, she did die in May.

She was so thrilled when my sister was born, and she remembers much more about her than I do. She was the first born Jewell girl in many generations. Strange to think, that there have been so many Jewell girls since then. I'm a father to three myself, and from what I've been told of Myngu Norman was as strong a character as mine are turning out to be.

If Myngu found a penny, she'd put it down the drain, instead of keeping it or passing it on to someone else. Myngu feared no one and would walk to town every day through the lanes behind the rows of terraced houses because it was quicker. One Christmastime, before I was born, and my brother was a toddler, she was attacked and robbed while walking back laden with bags and presents including a Black plastic horse for my brother. He stole her bag, including her purse and her house keys. She had a hell of a shock, battered and bruised and lost her confidence for a while.

Years later, and Myngu long gone to her grave, Dycu had someone trying to let themselves into his house one night.

They thought that they had a key for the door but Bill had changed the locks a long time before and was undisturbed by the attempt at entry, but it raised the question as to whether or not myngu's attacker had known where she lived and had followed her home.

Myngu, like many women of her generation, wore wigs. A fashion which is slowly returning so my girls tell me. Myngu's last wig came from some catalogue and arrived after her death, and was returned under the sad circumstances.

Myngu loved ghost stories and any films on the television that would frighten her. While I was sitting with my father one evening watching telly, a film came on that I thought he'd enjoy watching. It was a horror film in black and white, and from its description I doubted that he'd need to go out to sort the dog in the middle of it either. "I'd rather not," was his comment when I suggested it, "That's the film that Myngu watched the night she died." Apparently, Myngu had stayed up late to watch this film, and had suffered a massive heart attack and died in her bed. Myngu's death was a terrible and unexpected shock to us all. She left us all so suddenly, without even a goodbye. Dad like his brothers felt the loss greatly, and Dycu was left alone and lost without his life companion to mourn the death of such a wonderful person.

As I remember Dycu, he was a widower who never quite came to terms with losing his love. He was very much loved within his community, as a kind and helpful old gent, who'd cut people's lawns. His own back garden was always perfectly lawned with a flourish of colour around its borders. He had a concreted front garden as it failed to get any sun and he admitted defeat in trying to grow anything there.

He'd spend much of his time during the summer months, standing on his front doorstep, arms behind his back, watching the world pass by. Everyone who passed him would greet him. Some said a quick "Hello" as they made their way to town and others who'd pause for a chat as they made their way home from shopping. Dycu Bill had a smile for everyone and met each cheery gaze with a salute of his hand from his position on the front door. They'd never come further than the gate, and they'd hang their arms over the gate while they caught up on all the latest news. Dycu Bill got to know much more than I would ever get to know from my community, and he was discretion itself with certain people and their certain stories.

It wasn't only the grown-ups that used to chat with Dycu either. He was a kindly "Mr Jewell" to a few generations of kids who'd pass or even call for sweets off him. A very different time where suspicion was never at the forefront of anybody's mind should a kind old gentleman offer a child sweets. They were nearly always Humbugs or "losin dant" from Collins on the market in Llanelli. Even when he could no longer go shopping by himself the list that Mam would get would include sweets for the local children.

Dycu Bill, like my dad, and I'd like to think, me, was a people person. He loved talking to people and saw the best in people. Dycu had built a good name for himself too, as a generous character who'd always help if he could. From an early age, my wish was to grow up to be like him and like my dad. I'm still trying to achieve this through Dycu and Dad, the bottom lip can lead to an explosive temper sometimes.

His house in Lakefield Road was painted White on the outside with woodwork painted in baby pink. His front gate was white too with "Hazeldene" in pink block letters. Inside hadn't altered much since myngu's time there. The parlour was almost never used, and the television sat mute and unused. The middle room was a dark room with a massive mural of the Rockies covering the whole of the chimney wall.

I very much regret never sitting him down and asking him to go through his time in Canada with me in detail, but as a child, things like that seemed irrelevant to everyday life.

His kitchen was white and red and would be very retro in today's fashion. He had a gas cooker, and a coal stove to warm the kitchen and the water. Dycu would spend most of his day in the kitchen, in his low comfy chair by the kitchen table, with Radio 4 playing in the background. I used to laugh that Dycu used to listen to the dramas on Radio 4, but as I get older I love listening to them especially if I'm travelling in the car between work appointments. He didn't own a fridge but had a cool cupboard in the lean-to which led out of the house in the back, and he kept things cool in there. He'd always have ideal milk, and ate a diet of tinned and fresh food.

I don't ever remember him buying a daily newspaper, but he did get the Llanelli Star every Thursday without fail, in order to catch up with any news he'd possibly missed and subscribed to the monthly Readers Digest. He was the only person that I've ever met that subscribed to the Readers Digest!

As he got older, he started liking more gawdy and bright colours. Dad returned from visiting him one day, to say that Dycu Bill had painted the passage of the house in orange and purple. He became very lonely after becoming ill, and as he couldn't stand out to see people, he bought himself a Jack Russell puppy, and for some obscure reason, called him Terry to begin with before changing his name to Spot. He loved that crazy little dog and Dycu spoilt him.

Each year on January the 26th, Dycu would remember his wife's birthday and tended to bring out the booklet which showed the details of her cremation. One year the postman called, and while he was showing the document to the postman, the dog ran through the front gate and got killed by a passing car. Spot died on her birthday, which made the remembrance of that day even more poignant from then on. My father buried the dog's remains in the deep border at the back of Dycu's garden, and Dycu went back to his loneliness. Someone then gave him a cat, who he adored, though the cat was extremely temperamental with people but adored Dycu Bill.

Years later, and with our family now living in Dycu's old home, we had a new dog after losing Whisky, and Ben the beautiful long haired ginger sheepdog came into the kitchen carrying something in his mouth. Dad buried Spot's head for the second time that day, but a lot deeper this time.

We all felt the loss of losing Dycu Bill when he went. The community had long been used to seeing him around, on his doorstep willing people to stop and chat as they passed. I'd neglected him quite a bit in the past few months as I discovered friends in the area and took him for granted and hadn't visited him for months.

Uncle Norman, Aunty Sheila and the kids lived in Pen Coed, Bridgend, and Norman had said that he was calling down to see him. When Norman arrived, he walked into the house and dycu Bill said, "Norman, it's good to see you," before collapsing and dying in Norman's arms. We believe to this day that he'd waited long enough to see Norman one final time before going.

Norman came up to our house, to tell us of Dycu Bill's death, and Mam was immediately reminded of a similar experience that she had when Norman rushed up to the house on the 8th of May, 1969 to tell us that Myngu'd gone. Norman took the cat back with him and though it remained a very independent cat, it was with them for years.

Chapter 11
My Dad's Relations

Ray Tumble

One of the most colourful characters on my father's side of the family was Ray Tumble. Until today, I don't honestly know for sure how we were related to her but I think that she was one of Winnie's cousins. Ray was a woman who always looked amazingly smart and elegant. Of short stature with extra-large glasses, full makeup, bright lipstick and bouffant hair, I always thought that she looked like a film star when we'd meet her in town shopping. She belonged to the wigs and full makeup era, though it took me a while to understand that it wasn't her own hair. She was older than Daddy, and Dad remembered her as a stunningly pretty girl when they were young. She was related to us through Gwilym Coran somehow. Dad always said that Ray was posher than they were when they were younger. Dad and his family were living in Tumble by then and Ray and her mother Blod lived in Upper Tumble no less. The difference in Social status within a small coal mining community obvious and well recognised locally. Blod took in lodgers who worked in the local mines, and Uncle Ken, Dad's older brother, always used to repeat the story that Blod's lodgers would never go out on a Friday night with the other workers after a hard week's graft because Friday night was bath night for a very pretty 17-year-old Ray in a tin bath in front of the fire. The lodgers would find reasons to walk into the kitchen while she was there and excuse themselves for interrupting at an alarming rate.

Ray always spoke amazingly posh too. I always remember how she'd greet my mam, "Haaaaaazel" she'd say in Welsh, "how aaaaaaaare yooou?" Her Welsh was perfect, with an accent that was difficult to recognise, but not like our broad Llanelli accent, and she spoke like she had money in the bank. Her clothes, like her accent and her make-up and her hair were just so. Every inch of her had been worked to perfection in the mirror before coming out of the house to go shopping I always thought.

We'd almost always find Ray in Marks and Spencer when it was located in Llanelli town Centre opposite Woolworths. M&S suited her style, and if Mam started talking to her there, we could be there for hours. She always had pictures of Jane and John in her bag. These were her children, older than us, that I never met but always admired their lifestyle as reported by their proud Mam.

We'd often hear stories about Winnie, and how endearing a character she was, and how kind she'd been with Blod before she died so suddenly. We'd get to hear all about her exotic Holiday adventures too, or to London to stay with Jane or her trips on the Orient Express. "What's that?" asked my mother once and having had the answer off Ray, Mam went on to say that she "didn't like trains"! somehow, Ray and the luxury Orient Express went hand in hand.

The workers at Marks and Spencers knew her well, and if they had the time, they'd spend time chatting with her while she shared snip bits from her family's memoirs, mention wonderful places and more than anything, showed her Cartier watch to them. In an age of false makes and cheap replicas, Ray's Cartier watch was the real thing. Her watch, like clothes and her love of expensive things, recognised that her husband Alcwyn was a successful International business manager and though they lived in Llanelli as we did, they came from a different world.

****

Arthur and Mary Jewell, Burry Port

Arthur was one of Dycu Bill's Brothers, and he was married to Mary from rural Ireland, though I never met her. Arthur was a very smartly dressed man who had a 1950s moustache. He looked like a bit of a cad from the St Trinian's movies if I'm honest. Arthur drove a two-tone blue Rover 100 that he took great pride in, and it shined as though it was brand new. Arthur would choose carefully which days he'd come to visit Bill. If it promised rain then the car stayed in the garage clean and dry. Rain was not going to spoil the shine on that car.

I'd often see Arthur when we'd go down to see Dycu Bill. He was always extremely witty, and he like Bill had learnt to speak a Llanelli Welsh, though his English remained from far away.

Arthur'd experienced a sad past too, and during the second world war, he refused to join the army and therefore brought shame on to his relations and family. I'd often heard talk that Arthur was a "conchy", but had never quite realised what the name meant in reality. "Conscientious objectors," was the name given to men who refused call up to the armed forces, and cited religious convictions for doing so. At the time, there were some who genuinely believed that the Scriptures did not agree with war and others who saw this as an excuse to avoid going away to get killed.

I can honestly say, hand on heart, that I'd be with that second group, and that I'd have followed Uncle Arthur in his shame.

Being a "conchy" didn't make life much easier either in the long run, and throughout the war, Arthur worked in the Ammunitions Factory down Pembrey. The work was dangerous and difficult, and the risk of hurt was real enough. Added to that of course, was the ridicule and negative reaction to him that he would have suffered for not going to fight like the other men in Burry Port.

Mary on the other hand was the complete opposite of Arthur. A rural, poor, Irish girl with a strong Irish accent who was going blind as I was growing up. Dad remembered going to see her at home many years before and was surprised by how poor they lived. Not enough cups to offer one each, and having to use jam jars to get a cup of tea. The house was a shambles, which was hard to believe seeing that Arthur was so immaculately turned out always while Mary sat at home.

****

Tom and Dilys Jewell of the Cawdor Arms, Llandeilo –

Tom was Dycu Bill's eldest brother, and we'd sometimes get to meet him in Dycu's house. Tom was known for having a high opinion of himself, and he'd married Dilys Gray who was very English. When they'd call, we'd get to sit in the parlour. This was Dycu's best room and was hardly ever used, apart from when "visitors" came. I don't remember too much about Tom, only that he had big sticking-out ears and his wife was very thin and like a Chinese porcelain doll with white makeup which made her look like a ghost. They never had any children, and from my memory of them, had very little interest in us as children either. They lived above the Cawdor Arms in Llandeilo for years.

The Grays from the border towns of Wales were Dilys's family, and Tom possibly thought that he'd married well. Apparently, when they married, he failed to invite his own mother for fear of embarrassing himself and his new wife because of his mother's working-class nature. Dilys certainly saw herself as an important woman within her society of friends.

Dycu Bill would always laugh at her when she called. There was always a great waft of scent when she arrived, which filled the room, and when she sat in the parlour in the armchair behind the door, Dycu would be on the other side in the passage making shapes and making us laugh.

Tom wasn't popular within our family, and Uncle Ken couldn't stomach him at all. I don't know all the story, but from what I remember being told when Ken married Audrey and started a family, they set up home in a house that Tom Jewell owned called Alberta. It was a house on the end of a row opposite the avenue in Llwynhendy, named after the district in Canada where Ken was born. But Tom threw Ken and Audrey and the young family out for some reason leaving them homeless. The situation created a lot of ill-feeling, and if Uncle Ken was alive today, his top lip would not be able to hide his disgust towards Tom Jewell.

The one thing I remember most about Dilys was the time when she phoned Dad to tell him that Tom Jewell had died. Tom was getting on a bit, and news of his death was not completely unexpected. After coming off the phone, Dad let his two brothers know the news he'd been given. In order to find out the arrangements for the funeral, Norman phoned Dilys back to offer condolences. Tom answered the phone! Dilys was also getting on a bit by now too and her mind was not what it had been. Tom was very much alive and lived a good few years to continue his life of snobbery.

****

Uncle Wil

Will was Myngu Norman's brother. A confirmed bachelor by nature, Will enjoyed life down the Labour Club and had only himself to worry about. Will was always extremely nice to us kids and loved the fact that we were Elwyn's kids. Will had moved in to live with Dycu Bill after Myngu'd died for him to have some company but it was not a match made in heaven. Will lived in the tiny box room and had very few possessions. Dycu had kept Myngu's room as it had been before she died, and he opted to sleep in the back bedroom.

I always remember Will as a small, thin, innocent-looking old man, who was always glad to see us. He spoke with a kind, meek voice, and was always getting coal to feed the stove in the kitchen. Dycu Bill really threw his weight around in front of us too. He got on Dycu Bill's nerves, and Will put up with so much negativity off him and never answered him back. He'd be accused of being useless, and his annoyance at the situation that Dycu Bill found himself in was taken out on Will. Poor uncle Will. His only sanctuary was the Labour Club on a Friday night, and then spent the rest of the week trying to keep out of Bill's way.

Dad really liked Uncle Will, and always told the story of a wild weekend that they'd had I Galway, Ireland with the boys in the 50s before Dad was married with a wicked smile.

They must have been some sort of company for each other at one point, but when Dycu became ill with prostate cancer the first time and was in the hospital a while, Dad and the others were told by Bill that Will needed to find an alternative place to live.

It's quite possible that Dycu was worried that he'd die and that Will would be a sitting tenant in the house that he'd left them in his will and that the boys wouldn't want to move him from there. By the time that Bill had come out of the hospital, Will had found himself an old age bungalow down the road from Dycu's house, and although Dad used to call to see Will from time to time, Will never did step foot in Lakefield again, and never did see Bill again, though he did come to see him off at Bill's funeral.

The Part 3
The Bonkers Years

The physical, social, and educational influences that hit me like a ton of bricks as I reached my teenage years and ahead.

Chapter 12
The Influence of Physical Changes!

I'd always known that I was a big lad. I'm often called a "big kid" now but that's possibly because of my refusal to take things seriously. My clothes had been for an adult size since I was around ten and not a skinny adult either! Though tall enough not to stick out and look seriously like Ken Dodd's beloved diddy men of my childhood, on the streets of my home town, the fact that my waist was seriously bigger than what was considered normal, required visits to Reginald Watson gents outfitters with my mother, whenever I needed a pair of 32 short leg trousers, much to my shame prior to reaching my teens.

To be fair, they were nice enough there, straight out of "Are you being served ?" but for a shop that seemed to target elderly American Golfers, having to wear green and red check trousers to school for the week was enough to haunt me for years. I remember damning that there wasn't a school uniform rule in force at Ysgol Dewi Sant when I was there.

It's a good laugh to look back at our classroom pictures from that era. Everyone in their best clothes for the last school picture in Form 4. Miss Tomos in one of her chapel frocks, John Morris Williams, with a smart suit and a seriously red face, and Marks and Spencer's apparently the chosen shop for knitted tops in various colours for the girls. Some of my classmates were maturing earlier than others, and I stand all smiles in my brown tie and cream shirt with a matching cardigan, and the smile was probably there because I was in the back and could hide my green plaid golfing check slacks!

By the start of the years of great change, the wearing your best clothes to Sunday school had disappeared along with the effort to go on Sundays too, but as I still hadn't had the chance to choose my own clothes, they remained very respectable and almost always brown.

Mam knitted me jumpers for years, and they never had to show any label that allowed people to know my size. She was good at knitting too, and quite happy to do it as long as we didn't ask for any cableing or Fairisle! Mam grew out of knitting itchy balaclavas too, much to my relief! I'd been forced to wear them for years over Winter, and that wirey wool played havoc with my "putty-faced" complexion. Fair play to her, she kept on creating jumpers for me through my college days, without worrying about how much wool they took to knit, and the fashion of the 80s called for mohair which attracted all sorts of comments, good and bad. Overnight my mother's commentary changed too and the "don't be silly it's only puppy fat" replaced with "Good god Robert you need to stop eating. I'm sure that you've got eating diabetes"

Until I reached my college days, and was told differently, I always had thought that "Eating Diabetes" was in fact a real affliction and not just a term created by my mam for anyone who scoffed too much!

I've always thought of this growing period in my life as the time when my body finally started catching up with the size of my head! I got taller and my feet got much bigger just as the big new Tesco Store opened in town. On the site of what is Tinopolis now, the biggest Tescos that I'd ever experienced opened and they had clothes that fitted me there.

They also had the smell of freshly cooked bread pumping through the Entrance Hall, but that's another story. Navy blue cords were my first independent purchase, with a blue check brushed cotton shirt and navy tank top to match. No sign of golfers' trousers anywhere. I'd finally arrived in the real world, and would be going to Ysgol y Strade in September 1978.

I now had a bit more control over what I'd wear from now on, and few pairs of jeans and even a green parker with a fur rimmed hood followed – the height of fashion for me at the time. I never did become a kid who liked expensive labels. I was just glad that normal sizes were fitting me at last.

"I don't know who you think you are?" would be the normal comment from my mother, "No one's going to be looking at you!" and I absorbed it all. I finally started to realise that I needed to not only look after my developing self but protect myself from an ever judgmental mam on my way to becoming a grown-up.

Vincent Morris the clothes shop was also a good way of getting quality clothes and paying every week "on tick" especially when there was a Sale there – Dad and Mam working hard so that I could start to feel that I was standing on my own two feet, but with their cash of course. I honestly don't know how they managed it all, especially when you consider that I was the youngest of three.

I'd have liked to say that the physical changes would have brought on changes to my voice too, but that remained melodically effeminate and I continued to succeed in winding other boys up just by talking or even just being there. David my husband laughs now, as when I say hello to any man passing us on the road, I suddenly become this gruff workman type with the lowest voice you'd ever hear.

My hairstyle was straight out of the seventies, and over my ears, as fashion dictated. I'd go to Upper Park Street opposite the long gone Stepney Hotel to get my hair cut on a Saturday. "Man at the Top" I think it was called, with Mam sitting behind me and watching every movement of the scissors from start to finish. I don't remember the barber's name, only that he was tall and thin and wore cool sunglasses in the shop. He was long-haired in the Starsky and Hutch fashion and wore high waist-banded flairs.

It was always busier there in the mornings and I never understood for years, that the haircut was always tidier then than in the afternoon. Allegedly it was known, that the guy'd have a couple of pints in the Tŷ Melyn Hotel on a lunchtime, and haircuts became certainly more avant-garde by the afternoon.

Having a "widow's peak" in the front of my hair never promised to get the best of styles with my hair, but I'd try hard to look like the heroes of the age. Showing my ears remained for the time being, like something that belonged to my early childhood.

Chapter 13
Changes in Social Influences

The summer of 1978 was an important period for me socially. I got the chance to start finding myself and finding what the world outside the house had to offer me. The rules that governed my decisions, my individuality, my determination to keep out of trouble and even my ability to think for myself were firmly in place by then. It hadn't always been easy for my parents to get me to understand this but their groundwork along with my Primary School was robust enough for my survival.

Overnight, I changed from being this quite solitary kid who sang to himself and broke "wild rubarb" from the bank to play with the kids next door, Only years later did I realise that this was actually Japanese knotweed that I snapped and threw like spears to everywhere.

Overnight, my name changed too. No longer Robert the would-be Prime Minister, but Jewell to all that knew me. I was more than delighted to be rid of that "Robert" for good. To this day, when someone calls me Robert, I'm immediately returned to the scorn and shame that accompanied it by my mam.

Deep down I suppose that Mam had been well meaning in her attempts to protect me from the kids around me. They'd all attended the same school and there wasn't a word of Welsh between them but being in their company was a breath of fresh air to me and a great relief. I was a boy from the "Welsh School" and as such knew how to behave.

Having said this, during this time, I learnt to smoke and swear, and more importantly, was accepted by them. Maybe Mam was right in her reluctance to allow me to let the apron strings go, but I never looked back.

As in all other times of my life, I naturally got on better with the girls than the boys, but fair play to them, it wasn't often that I felt out of place especially considering that my world could feel so very different from theirs at times.

We went through a long stage of sitting on the steps of the corner shop, talking nonsense for hours. Walking down to the beach was always a pleasant experience and one which allowed me to get to know the others better. There'd be arguments and name-calling at times as in any group of friends, and maybe there'd be people ignoring each other or "not Friends". But at the end of the day, for the first time in my life, I became part of that normal "nonsense"

Relationships became extended with some – Nicola and Jonathon going out with each other for what seemed like years, and me still trying so hard to make sure that no one saw my true feelings towards anyone.

My new friends weren't young people that my family wholeheartedly approved of, especially as they were the ones who kept Aunty Phil in business and who stole from the sweet shop.

I do remember Jonathon telling his mam and dad that he was going on a School trip once. John's dad was a policeman, but John was no angel. He kept the money that had been given to pay for the trip with the intention to hide in Nicola's shed in the back garden for three nights.

He lasted a night, of course, before Nicola's parents realised that Nicola had become very interested in her dad's shed.

I was great friends with John, especially as he was so very different from me, doing things that my "grounding" would never allow me to consider. Lately, and with the whole of Wales between us, we have managed to re-connect, proving that years and miles count for nothing when there's a bond between friends.

Once he phoned me in panic. I could hear it in his voice. He'd taken his hamster out of the cage and had lost him in his bedroom. Would I come over and help him look for it? Between the first phone call and the next one, I'd managed to find my shoes and was about to start from the house. Less panic this time, but more pitiful. John had found his hamster alright, by stepping back he'd accidentally crushed it with his foot.

This motley crew's membership changed from time to time, through fighting and finding new friends. What was always a constant was how the friends that called for me were always left sitting on the step waiting for me if I wasn't ready. They were never invited in.

Dad "lost it" completely once, when he realised that the boys who were on the step waiting for me had been playing with matches, and had pushed one into our front door lock rendering it useless. I would have denied their involvement if I could have done for fear of losing their friendship.

The guilty boy was made to pay for a new lock for the front door. They could certainly afford it as their house was huge compared to ours. Things were never quite the same between me and that friend after that.

Isn't it strange the things that come to mind when you think right back? Another time we went to a friend's house where he encouraged us to look around his dad's home office. I was given what I thought were old brass rifle cases.

Later that evening, his dad appeared on our doorstep, asking whether or not we still had the live bullets. I'd arranged them neatly on the mantlepiece to match my mother's other brass ornaments. His face dropped when he saw them there, warming nicely above the fire. Another reason why my dad so disliked this particular friend!

I was lucky in being able to keep my social life and my other life separate. I never got into any serious trouble as a teenager, and being the size I was had its advantages – I could buy "twenty bensons" easily without any questions about my age, though not from Aunty Phil of course.

I was allowed to go to my first disco at 13. A Parish Hall Disco no less. To say that I was apprehensive would be a grave understatement, I was absolutely "bricking" it. It was before I had met any new friends, and I'd guessed that no one from my school would be there. Why I'd ever insisted on going is beyond me, especially as I knew no one, couldn't dance and didn't have appropriate clothes to go. But I went. Met a very good-looking boy with deep brown eyes who like me felt very odd there. He sat with me. He was kind and chatty and I left there, glad of knowing that I had a new friend, one that understood me. He lived in the Old Lodge Council flats Estate, not too far from me. I can't for the life of me, remember his name but when Mam asked me if I'd enjoyed it when I got home, I could honestly say that I had.

I didn't see him again for a few years, and though I am ashamed to say it when I did see him whilst in the company of my friends, I denied that I knew him. I still hate myself for that denial. The problem which I could not face up to at that age was the fact that he had come out as gay at a young age, and my desperate attempts to hide the real me from my friends would never allow me to befriend him. He was gay and he was bullied for it, and though I was also bullied horribly for that very reason, being in that great big Egyptian river (Denial) helped me to somehow fool myself.

What was handy about being bigger than most and looking older than I was was the fact that I could get into the Classic cinema in town to see films rated 18. Me and Nicola from next door but one would often go and no one would question our ages. Who reading this, remembers Koo Stark, Randy Andy's one-time girlfriend? Or Sylvester Stallone's first attempt at the movies as the "Italian Stallion" – All I will say is that he was quite "ordinary" from what I can recall or they'd possibly filmed certain scenes with no heating on!

This was all part of growing up, and the reasoning, the chatting, the "serious" discussions and the comparing on all levels all part of developing my personality.

It was a time for roller skates and "Roller discos" in the Glen by the Town Hall. Remarkably, I wasn't too bad on them, but when I fell I fell hard and heavy. The same could not be said when it comes to skateboarding which I hoped would pass quickly as a faze!

With my new found friends, at least I had someone to chat with when the boys wanted to play footie! Left-footed and terrified of proving once and for all that I had very little coordination, I avoided any offers to "have a game"

If ~I did have to play, I'd always opt for goalie with the hope that they were much better than the other team. I wanted the least possible contact with a ball that I could.

We had no mobile phones or any electronic pocket devices at all. But the roads were safe enough to wander about in the evening without any real worry.

Of course, all this changed on the discovery of poor Amanda Randall's remains in Felinfoel in 1978. She was a fourteen-year-old school girl from the Bigyn area and died in horrendous circumstances. What's more is that Aunty Ann, Uncle David and the kids lived up the road from her and knew the family well. We didn't know her. She was older than us and didn't go to our schools but her death left an impression on us all – life wasn't as safe as we'd thought it to be.

During the long Summer holidays, I wouldn't see any of my School friends at all. My local friends and I would stroll down to the beach or maybe further at times. Stradey Castle Woods was always a great place to have a laugh and mess about in an innocent way, before being chased off the land by the gamekeeper. Some of the gang were cheekier than others though no one was a concern to the others.

I was growing up and we'd discuss all sorts of things in our shared quest to understand the world a bit better. I continued to hide my true me, though in reality, on contemplation, I was really fooling no one but myself. When times became heated, and accusations about my sexuality were made, I'd retreat back to the safety and sanctuary that my back garden had to offer. During times like that I really hated who I was and I would desperately try to work out why it was so wrong to be me.

Having licked my wounds, I would eventually get back out there, to take another shot at surviving the world.

As we got older, the gang divided into smaller interest groups. I spent my O-level revision days on the step of one of the two Sharons testing each other on what we'd just learned. In reality, there wasn't much revision but it felt better than nothing and it got me out of the house.

By then, we'd moved into my grandfather's house down the road, and to the middle of the excitement that was Lakefield Road. It had its plus points though hearing the laughter that followed my mother shouting down the road to come in was not one of them. The shame was horrible but I was used to it by then.

My life changed again at the end of the Summer of 1983. While my friends started working, I returned to the 6th form the gang was split up forever and friends from my early childhood were once more a part of my social life as the pubs and clubs opened up to us.

What was interesting then and is still as fitting now, is that I had many different groups of friends who knew nothing of each other. Compartmentalised into boxes, I'd never think that they would ever meet let alone get on with each. A social butterfly, all be it an overweight one, flitting from one group of friends to the other and never the twain shall meet. I could happily order a selection of cakes for an afternoon tea with Menna and Siân at the Jenkins Cafe in town, on the one hand, while buying 20 Bensons and 4 Cans of Strongbow to drink down the beach that evening with another group.

It's been the same throughout my life so far, and I see no hint of it ever-changing.

Chapter 14
The Influence of Educational Changes

There is so much talk about how teenage boys' feet smell. As I grew older my feet never smelled at all for the simple reason that sport and exercise were never a meaningful part of my life. From that first shame of the showers after rugby with my strategically placed flannel to hide from the other boys as per my mother's wishes to landing in the middle of the horse in gymnastics and crying in front of everyone. I shake my head when I think of gymnastics as a School sport for everyone, but in all honesty, who would ever consider me a candidate for gymnastics at all?

I guess that after my attempts at being a prop forward in green flash daps, I recognised that I'd need an excuse to never ever have to do it again. The answer, of course, was an "in growing toenail" and fair play to my mother, in writing that repetitive note on a weekly basis. "Jewell, don't even tell me "was Lyn gym's weekly comment, though sometimes I did have my uses. Normally as the person, he trusted to clean out his locker room on a regular basis. I won't even begin to discuss what this did to a pubescent boy with sexuality confusion.

Must admit that I had my share of pretty horrible bullying while at Secondary School. It was much worse than I'd ever experienced in Primary School. "Poof" or similar was the chosen words. I never told my parents about them or my mam would have probably blamed me for it! But I hardened my attitude towards them – wasn't it true what they said about sticks and stones? Sometimes, though, it was physical, and at those times I tried hard to do what Mam and Dad said and "just walk away".

"You're not supposed to talk English in the Welsh School" was probably the single most ridiculous thing I could have told anyone ever in Welsh on my first day of Secondary School. I said it and believed it that first day and aimed it towards a group of girls from my year.

What was worse is that the very boys who had come to my birthday party when I was younger had now found a voice to torment me and make my life hell. I was an easy target to other boys. I'd never hit back and I'd never report it. An overweight, effeminate boy, with a voice like Charlotte Church who enjoyed folk dancing, choir singing, soloing and duetting as a soprano and who hated any sport but especially rugby in a School that was known for its turn out of successful players. Coupled with this was my mother's insistence that I wear the biggest leek I could find for St David's Day only to get it ripped off and beaten with once I got to School.

One year, as was customary on St David's Day, the School had an Eisteddfod. A chance for the musically gifted or poetically minded to shine on March the 1st. I was there to sing like a canary on steroids in head to toe yellow, representing my School House, namely Madog who was always represented by yellow. I was in form 2 and my opponent that day was the ruggedly handsome rugby playing, charm from form 4 that was Duncan. A very popular competitor from the screams of the love-bitten girls in the back of the school hall. From the hollering alone, Duncan certainly had won already and he hadn't opened his mouth yet. The Judge for the day's competitions was Hywel Teifi Edwards whose wife was the wonderful Madog house leader, and sport and craft teacher Aerona Edwards.

The competition was the Open Folk song for boys – I sang The Sol-fa song in Welsh though had some serious problems with various letters due to my aforementioned inability to pronounce certain letters.

I was willing Duncan to win, like most of the audience, but his performance along with the fact that the now-famous newsreader Huw Edwards's father was not only the Judge and the House Leader's son but my brother's friend through the Llanelli Young Music Lovers. Of course with a surname like Jewell and a bulky stature like my brother, he was bound to favour me. Yes, I indeed did win, but it was very much an empty victory and I swore then and there that I'd never put myself in such a vulnerable situation again.

I was always popular with the girls, though not in that way They trusted me and they shared their concerns and confidences with me. I've often said that I've always been a magnet to those who need to "talk". Over the years, I've developed a way of saying the truth however painful in an honest polite way. I was once described by a deputy head teacher as having the ability to "Kick ass with a smile on my face and in a way that no one gets offended". It's continued to be my strength and as a father to three girls, I call on it often to discuss and reason things through.

I learned a lot about how to understand different personalities too, and to this day, I seem to find that I can look at someone and quite successfully guess what sort of person he or she is too.

My world has always been filled with girls. Welsh Departments where I've worked in schools have a high percentage of women as does the teaching profession on the whole. I have also come to recognise that I seem "interesting" to a certain type and age of a woman who finds me "approachable". I guess it's down to the constant struggle I had to win over my mother's affections which never was successful.

With my life very much an open book these days, if you pardon the pun, and worries about my sexuality laid to rest, my friendship with women remains constant.

With the opportunity I've had to rekindle old and precious friendships, I've been able to reconnect and be honest. I'd kept away from some who I feared would accidentally out me when the time wasn't right for me.

Education certainly teaches you a lot about life. I learned a lot about other people during my time at School. I got to understand how to carefully step around some people, avoid others at all costs, but invest in the people that took to me. I've always said that the best influences you can have in life are good teachers and friends that are fair to you. I've experienced very many of those, and Facebook being the great connector that is, has allowed me to keep close contact with those who mean something to me.

In the same way, I've been able to use the skills that I've picked up along the way and can do my best with most people.

Like everyone else, I am a composite of life experiences both good and bad, of my upbringing and of my family both birth and chosen friends along the way.

To finish

Writing these memories has raised many thoughts that I'd long forgotten about and the whole experience has certainly been a cathartic one for me. I hope that you've enjoyed the stories both funny and sad, and that you haven't been too bored by them.

It was never my intention to scratch the scab off any experience, nor did I go out of my way to upset anyone by repeating my childhood stories, but if it did then, c'est la vie. Life is too short to worry!

I've purposefully not spoken too much about close family. I've concentrated on experiences and family that are no longer with us, but that was very much a part of my childhood.

As for me, I'm very content in my world by now, despite experiences that could have had a very negative impact on my character. I learnt to raise my own children by following my dad's pattern.

If I'm honest, I think that I tend to over-think things at times too. One of the difficulties of working with children's welfare and inclusion, child protection and safeguarding for so long, and noticing how the negative experiences hinder self-worth and self-growth in an individual.

Thank you for reading, and I do hope that you've enjoyed some of Llanelli's past too. I purposely left out the way that Llanelli people tend to drop the "h" from the start of each word so as not to confuse you too much. "I do 'ope that you're 'appy with that!

> Rob – Summer 2019

Post-script 2022

Proof reading this memoir has made me realise that without a suitable update of my current situation, the portrayed scenario is incomplete

Mam. Having suffered mam's toxic negativity for many years as considered in this book, I finally took the decision to break away from her hold in June 2019. I'd long recognised that though she herself had been getting older, her venom was no less potent.

Ridiculously, I finally saw the light when she declared in one of our daily phone calls on my way to work, two weeks before my youngest daughter's eighteenth birthday that she was no longer going to send birthday cards. This was her youngest grand-child who'd recently overcome major open heart surgery and I felt a great sense of wrong.

The anger in my heart for my daughter's perceived hurt was overwhelming and I decided there and then that such toxicity had no place in mine or my children's lives any longer and that the cycle of hurt and shame stopped here.

Coupled with this was her lingering refusal to accept that not only was her youngest son gay but he had married his partner in 2016 and that his situation was happily accepted by all around him

That morning on the way to work as I put down the phone , was a turning point in my life and the lives of my children. No longer did they have to face the negativity, the ridicule and the toxicity of a myngu who'd spent her life judging them.

We never spoke again, and in the middle of what became the Covid lockdowns I received only two messages from my sister regarding mam being in hospital. Each time I sent my love but explained that I wouldn't be able to travel down

Mam died on the 7th of December 2020, and I found out through a dear neighbour and childhood friend, quite by chance on Facebook 10 days later on my 54th birthday. Neither my sister nor my brother or their families had felt the need to tell me that my mam had died . She was cremated as per Covid rules on December the 18th, without invitation for me nor my three daughters to attend.

Had she lived, who knows whether or not the relationship between us could have been salvaged in some way? I loved her dearly, but had over the years been able to see through her negative disregard for me and my family.

All I do know, is that she died knowing that she had managed to create what she'd always strived for, a situation ,where her offspring were at odds with each other, and continue to be so.

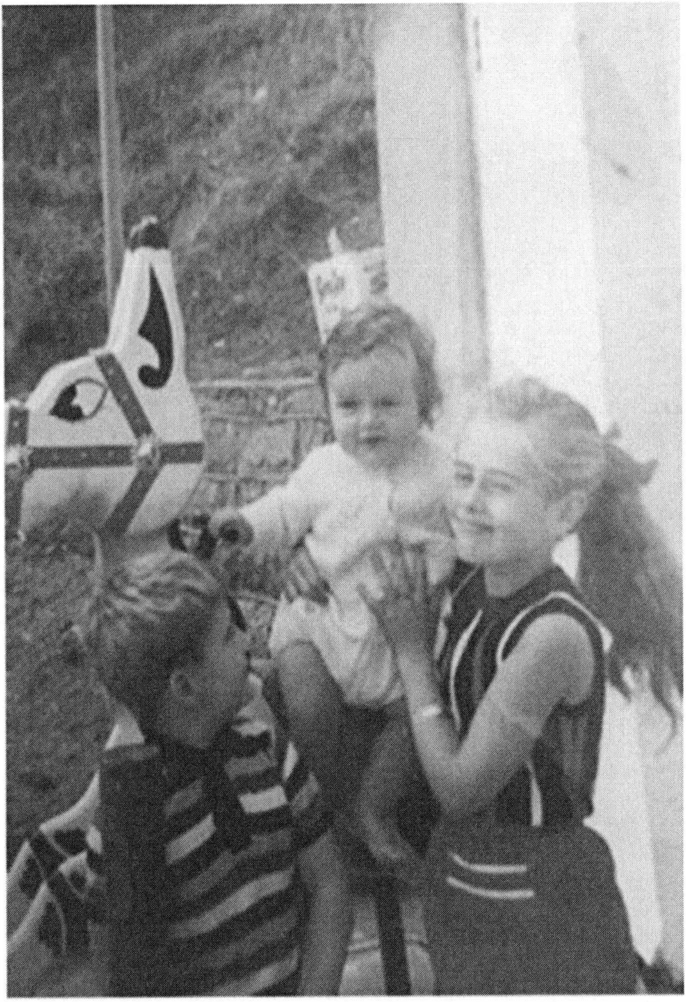